Few have seen angels. Fewer know how to activate angels to work on your behalf. Even fewer know how to release and mobilize your own angel. Now, for the first time, these will not be mysteries to you. Kevin Basconi has demystified angels.

**SID ROTH**
**Host, "*It's Supernatural!*"**

Kevin and Kathy Basconi are amazing forerunners in the Glory of God. Kevin has a language that articulates and defines the Glory of God that few I know have. Kevin's new book *Visitations of Angels and Other Supernatural Experiences* is filled with insight, testimony and revelation into the ministry and function of angels and will serve as a reference to who are looking to understand more into these realms.

I highly recommend this book to all who are hungry to understand the deep things of God

**JEFF JANSEN**
**Founder& Senior Leader, Global Fire Ministries International**

Kevin and Kathy Basconi's extraordinary supernatural experiences, revelation, and understanding of spiritual things have their basis in their urgent craving to know more of God; their consistent seeking and continuing communication and communion with Him; and their childlike, humble attitudes of openness to receive what He reveals to them. Add to that their continual desire and commitment to learn, their diligent search of the Scriptures, and their deliberate association with key individuals around the world who walk in a deeper level of communion with Jesus Christ of Nazareth.

From this deep and rich spiritual lifestyle of seeking and openness to hear and see both in earthly and in heavenly realms, the Lord has directed and enabled them to share their experiences and insights with the world; this time in this wonderful book,*Visitations of Angels & Other Supernatural Experiences Volume #1*. I consider it an honor and a privilege to know Kevin and Kathy as personal friends and partners in our spiritual walk throughout this world.

**DR. STEPHEN R. RICHARDSON**
**Ordained Foursquare minister and medical doctor, retired**

I am delighted to endorse *Angelic Visitations and Other Supernatural Experiences Volume #1* by Kevin Basconi. Kevin's life is established on a committed personal relationship with Jesus Christ. He knows the Holy Spirit intimately, and his encounters and revelations flow from this relationship and his diligent study of the Scriptures. I heartily recommend this book and Kevin Basconi to you.

*PATRICIA KING*
**Founder XP Ministries**


Wonderful! This book is full of wonder; it is overflowing in joy. Drink from the fountain of God's glory as you read it and walk away lighter and awestruck by His love! Experience His glory!

*JOAN HUNTER*
**Author - Evangelist**


Get ready! As you read this *Angelic Visitations and Other Supernatural Experiences Volume #1* by Kevin Basconi, it will be a supernatural treat! You will have the privilege of hearing from seasoned men and women of God and their interaction with angels. This is God's normal for you too! This is how the Lord interacted with His people in both the Old Testament and in New Testament and how He still interacts with people today! You will be brought into a new awareness of God's angels that are working all around you and learn how to cooperate with them as they do "Gods bidding". It's my pleasure to recommend *Visitations and Other Supernatural Experiences Volume #1* to you!

*ALAN KOCH*
**Christ Triumphant Church, Lee's Summit, Missouri**

# VISITATIONS OF
# ANGELS

## *& other*

## SUPERNATURAL
## EXPERIENCES

### VOLUME I

## KEVIN BASCONI

ISBN: 978-0-9960217-3-9

King of Glory Ministries International Publications 2015
King of Glory Ministries International
PO Box 903, Moravian Falls, NC 28654, 336-818-1210
www.kingofgloryministries.org

Unless otherwise noted, all scripture quotations are from the New King James Version of the Bible. Copyright © 1979, 1980, 1982 by Thomas Nelson, Inc., publishers. Used by permission.

Scripture quotations marked NASB are from the New American Standard Bible–Updated Edition, Copyright © 1960, 1962, 1963, 1968, 1971, 1972, 1973, 1975, 1977, 1995 by The Lockman Foundation. Used by permission. (www.Lockman.org)

Scripture quotations marked NIV are from the Holy Bible, New International Version. Copyright © 1973, 1978, 1984, 2010, 2011, International Bible Society. Used by permission.

Greek definitions are derived from Strong's Greek Concordance.

Hebrew definitions are derived from Strong's Hebrew Concordance.

Cover design & layout by Kevin Basconi and projectluz.com
Printed in the United States of America

This

book

Is

dedicated

to

*God the Father, God the Son, and God the Holy Spirit*

*without*

*You*

*Guys*

*none*

*of*

*this*

*would*

*have*

*been*

*possible!*

# Table of Contents

# Acknowledgements

I want to thank my wonderful precious wife, Kathy Basconi, for her everlasting love for me.

I want to let the world know that other than receiving Jesus Christ of Nazareth as my personal Savior and Messiah, Kathy is the most wonderful gift that my Father has ever given to me.

Thank you, Kathy, for all of your help with the books and other ministry projects.

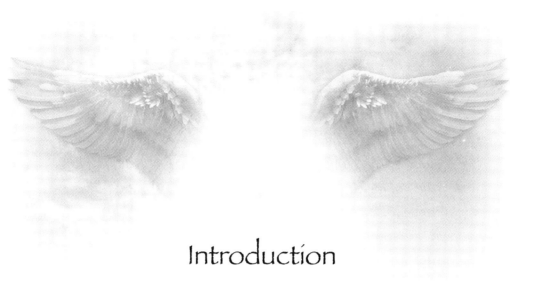

# Introduction

I pray that as you read these testimonies of angelic encounters they will be potential prophetic words for you according to the principle of Revelation 19:10, where it tells us, "*The testimony of Jesus is the spirit of prophecy.*" The Father has been gracious enough to allow me to see and discern God's angels and angelic activity for over a decade. And I pray that as you read this book it would activate something within your spirit and that the eyes of your heart or understanding would be enlightened. I pray that the gift of discerning of spirits would be activated in your life. And that you, too, would be able to recognize, discern, and see the angels of the Most High God who are actively working around each of us every moment of every day.

This supernatural ability is what I call the seer anointing.

I truly thank my heavenly Father that He has given us the authority and the privilege to co-labor with Christ's angels to manifest His Kingdom here on earth. We give Him all the praise and all the honor and all the glory in Jesus' might name.

The Book of Revelation says this: "*Then I heard a loud voice saying in heaven, 'Now salvation, and strength, and the kingdom of our God, and the power of His Christ have come, for the accuser of our brethren, who accused them before our God day and night, has been cast down. And they overcame him by the blood of the Lamb and by the word of their testimony, and they did not love their lives to the death'"* (12:10-11).

I believe as you read these testimonies about angelic encounters, they are potential prophetic promises for you to appropriate. I believe that our testimonies are powerful. As you read these testimonies, you can take them as potential open doors or supernatural gates for your life that may enable you to have similar supernatural encounters. If you press into the Kingdom of God, I believe you can have these same types of supernatural experiences.

Let me encourage you to pray the following prayer of reception before you begin reading this book. Pray the prayer of reception each time before you read this book and believe for the Spirit of the living God to release and activate your spirit. Believe for the Spirit of the Creator to minister to the spirit of the creature One on one. Believe to receive something amazing from the realms of heaven as you read *Angelic Encounters and Other Supernatural Experiences*. The Lord used angelic ministry and the mystical aspects of His Kingdom to initiate a supernatural metamorphosis in my life. I moved from poverty to prosperity, from sickness to health, and from hopelessness to hope. I also believe that God can activate and initiate a similar transformation in your life too.

Meditate and ponder upon these scriptures in your heart and then pray the prayer below.

**Ephesians 1:18:**

*The eyes of your understanding being enlightened; that you may know what is the hope of His calling, what are the riches of the glory of His inheritance in the saints.*

**1 Corinthians 2:9:**

*Eye has not seen, nor ear heard, Nor have entered into the heart of man The things which God has prepared for those who love Him.*

**Luke 8:10:**

*To you it has been given to know the mysteries of the kingdom of God, but to the rest it is given in parables, that "Seeing they may not see, And hearing they may not understand."*

**Hebrews 1:14:**

*Are they not all* (God's angels) *ministering spirits sent forth to minister for those who will inherit salvation?*

## Prayer of Reception

*Lord, I choose to believe to receive. Father, in Jesus' name, I purpose in my heart to believe to receive the prophetic promises that the Holy Spirit has placed into these pages. Lord, I am ready, I am willing, and I choose to receive everything that You are seeking to release to me from the Kingdom of Heaven through this book.*

*Holy Spirit, I ask that You would guide me and teach me. Lord, I ask that You would open my spiritual eyes and activate my spiritual ears to see and hear in a Christlike way. Lord Jesus, You said that to me it has been given and granted to know the hidden mysteries of the Kingdom of Heaven. Today, Lord, I choose to revive those blessings and revelations that You have hidden for me in the Holy Scriptures. Help me to see the keys to unlock the hidden mysteries of Your word and of Your Kingdom to me now. Lord, let Your Kingdom come into my life on earth as it is in heaven today.*

*I ask You to reveal to me the secrets and hidden mysteries that eye has not seen nor ear heard. Lord, I ask You to ignite my heart by Your Spirit and let the Kingdom of Heaven enter into my heart. Reveal to me the mysteries and the secret things that You have prepared for those who love You. I ask You, Father, in the name of Jesus, to reveal the fellowship of the mysteries and the unsearchable riches found in Christ to me. Reveal them to my spirit. O Lord, open my eyes to see the mysteries hidden in the Kingdom of Heaven. Lord, help me to discern the manifold wisdom of God. Lord, I am asking You to give me eyes to see and ears to hear in a new and supernatural way. In the name of Jesus Christ of Nazareth I pray. Amen!*

## CHAPTER 1

# Angels in the Heavenly Places

This testimony is about Jesus and the four angels in the heavenly realms. As a new believer, I began to seek the face of God earnestly and I began to pray because in my heart I knew God had a purpose for my life. So I began to fast and pray and ask Jesus about this every day. Shortly after I had been born again, I was in the middle of a water fast; I had been fasting and praying for approximately two weeks. Each day I would ask the Lord to tell me and reveal to me who I was and what kind of destiny that He had for me. You can rest assured that the Lord has a supernatural destiny that He has ordained for you to walk in too.

Through the work of the Holy Spirit, I just knew that God had a purpose for my life; and I earnestly sought Him to find out what this purpose was. I entered into a season of violently seeking the Kingdom of Heaven. This Scriptural principle is outlined in Matthew 11:12: *"And from the days of John the Baptist until now the kingdom of heaven suffers violence, and the violent take it by force."*

So when I speak of pressing into the Kingdom or violently taking the Kingdom, I am referring to this scriptural principle. What I really mean is that I sought the Lord with intense prayer accompanied with fasting. These types of fasts can take many forms. They can be true fasts, where one drinks only water for three to forty days. They can be a type of Daniel fast, where one only eats fruits and nuts along with drinking only juices and such. However, please allow me to encourage you to seek the Holy Spirit for His guidance on this kind of violent appropriation of the Kingdom of Heaven! The Holy Ghost knows best. Learn to allow the Holy Spirit guide you and teach you along these lines (John 16:13).

Having said all of this, allow me to say that prayer and fasting are two of the most important keys that can help you activate the eyes of your heart to learn to see and hear in a new and supernatural way. Prayer and fasting can help you activate the eyes of your understanding as we see the Apostle Paul outline in Ephesians 1: 15-21:

*Therefore I also, after I heard of your faith in the Lord Jesus and your love for all the saints, do not cease to give thanks for you, making mention of you in my prayers: that the God of our Lord Jesus Christ, the Father of glory, may give to you the spirit of wisdom and revelation in the knowledge of Him, the eyes of your understanding being enlightened; that you may know what is the hope of His calling, what are the riches of the glory of His inheritance in the saints, and what is the exceeding greatness of His power toward us who believe, according to the working of His mighty power which He worked in Christ when He raised Him from the dead and seated Him at His right hand in the heavenly places, far above all principality and power and might and dominion, and every name that is named, not only in this age but also in that which is to come.*

I have prayed this specific apostolic prayer almost daily for over a decade as of this writing. I believe that it is a key that can also help you unlock the heavenly realms for you too.

## Created in God's Image

Paul understood that we are created in God's image and that we all have a spiritual nature that we can step into. As we learn to exercise our spiritual senses by reason of use, we can learn to discern spiritual truths. We can learn to have the eyes of our understanding become dominant in terms of perception, and then we can be granted the grace by God to see into the spiritual dimensions! That is really what this book is all about! Your hope and calling is to be raised with Him and to be seated with Christ Jesus in the heavenly places. However, we must discern and learn to see such heavenly places and realms of glory.

My prayer is that as you read these testimonies that you would become inspired to seek the Kingdom of Heaven and to ask the Creator of the heavens and the earth, Elohim, to open up your spiritual eyes to see into His Kingdom. You see, our God is Spirit and He abides in a spiritual Kingdom. By the grace of God and the finished work of Jesus Christ on Calvary, we can learn to see into the Kingdom of Heaven. The Apostle John spoke of this character of the Lord in John 4:24: *"God is Spirit, and those who worship Him must worship in spirit and truth."* We can learn to discern heaven. We can learn to entertain heaven today.

Many times when the Lord begins to activate your spiritual senses or activate the eyes of your understanding it can be very subtle. So we need to learn to develop our sensitivity to the Holy Spirit as we grow and mature in this aspect of Christ's Kingdom (the seer anointing). Let me begin to share some testimonies that can help you to unlock these dynamics of the Kingdom of Heaven in your life and activate you to see and perceive God's angelic hosts who are actively working around us every waking moment. God commissions and sends forth His angels to work *"for"* you!

## Catapulted into Heaven

One day I was in my little house at 121 Beech Street in Blue-field, West Virginia, and I was praying in my little prayer closet. (Really, it was just a micro bathroom, about four feet by six feet.) I was lying there praying, when in the middle of my prayer I had a vision of Jesus. I was seeking the Kingdom of Heaven violently. I was pressing into the Lord.

I want you to catch this. I was not in a really fine or clean place. I was in a small dingy bathroom in a rundown little house in a drug-infested neighborhood. Here is a key for you to remember: it is all about the attitude of your heart and not your present circumstances. The Lord will meet you right where you are. The Lord looks at the heart, and Jesus is no respecter of persons (Acts 10:34). What Jesus did for me, He can do for you too. As I was praying and seeking the Lord in my little dingy bathroom, I was given a subtle vision.

In the vision I saw Jesus standing before me. He was waving at me with His arms, beckoning me to come toward Him. So in my mind I had a decision to make: I could either continue to pray to Jesus, or I could "go" to Him. I decided I wanted to go to Jesus (although I had no concept or grid of how or if I could actually "go" to the Lord). So I just purposed in my heart to "go." I was a new believer and I had never heard a lot teaching along this line. I had not read a lot of the Bible. I just thought that seeing Jesus and His angels was normal for a believer. I still do!

The very moment, the instant that I acquiesced and said, "Yes, Lord, I'll come," it felt as if I was being catapulted through time and space. I was launched out of my body, and I could feel my spirit man being taken up into the realms of heaven. After a couple of moments of ascending through the heavenly realms, I came to rest in the very presence of Jesus. When I did, I could feel the power of His unconditional love for me and I began to weep uncontrollably. I fell down upon my knees. I found myself on what appeared to be a pathway made of a golden substance.

This was amazing! And I was overcome with my surroundings and I seemed to be a bit like a fish out of water for a couple of moments as I sought to get my bearings. It was quite unsettling at first, but soon I started to feel perfectly at home and the peace of the God rested upon me.

After a few moments I looked up and I saw the Lord smiling at me with compassion. He was now standing right in front of me. I could feel His unconditional love. I also saw four angels who were standing with Jesus, just behind Him. They all had a powerful and holy presence attached to them. They had perfect smiles and were very strong. Three had long blonde hair and blue eyes, although one of the angel's eyes appeared to be blue green. Another seemed to have light sandy blonde hair or brown hair. They were all wearing beautiful spotless white robes that seemed to shimmer with phosphorescent supernatural colors. They also seemed to smell like heaven. In other words they smelled wonderful like frankincense and myrrh. At that moment two of the angels moved to my side and helped me to stand up. This both surprised and astonished me. The Lord Jesus stepped forward, and He looked deeply into my eyes.

It was the first time I had ever seen the eyes of the Lord; they are so beautiful, like pools of living love, pools of crystal clear living water. The Lord took His two nail-scarred hands and He placed them upon my shoulders. I could feel the power of His love surge through me again like 220 volts of electricity! It was amazing! The love of Jesus Christ is life changing! I could feel His unconditional love for all of mankind at that moment. Words cannot describe the eternal love of God that He pours out through this man named Jesus Christ of Nazareth, the Messiah. Truly, Jesus is the promised Savior of the world (John 3:16).

Jesus looked deeply into my eyes and He said, "Kevin, today I am going to tell you who you are." And this, of course, was the answer to my ongoing prayer. Jesus said, "I have called you to be an artist, and author, and an evangelist." When He said that, the power of His words penetrated to the very depth of my spirit. His words penetrated into the very fiber of my being, and I was changed. In a moment and in the twinkle of an eye I was transformed into a new creation at the word of the Lord. One legitimate word from heaven can transform your life and initiate a supernatural metamorphous of your character. The Lord's words resonated within me, and I knew with absolute certainty that is who God had created me to be. Before I was knit together in my mother's womb, God had in mind this purpose for me.

As I was thinking about this, I was feeling the unconditional love of Christ as it washed over me in waves. I could hear the sounds of harps and lutes and ethereal worship around me. There was like a white glory cloud that seemed to envelope us. Because of that I couldn't see very far, but I sensed that we were in an expansive place. In my mind I hoped that I would be given the opportunity to explore this place one day. As this thought matriculated into my spirit, I saw the Lord smile at me as if to say, "Of course, you are always welcome here." Later I would learn that you don't always have to use words to communicate in the heavenly realms. You see, in the spiritual or heavenly places our thoughts shout louder that our spoken words do upon the earth.

I could also see the angels who were in attendance. I took my eyes off the Lord to look these four angels over when the Lord spoke to me again. At that moment Jesus took His right hand and with a graceful sweeping motion He indicated the four angels who were standing behind Him. He said, "Kevin, today I'm assigning these angels to your ministry."

In my mind I was astonished; because I was a new believer, I didn't know I had a ministry. Almost immediately as I

questioned what the Lord had said, I found myself being hur-
tled back through time and space. I found myself back in my
little prayer closet at 121 Beech Street. I was weeping, and
I continued to feel the unconditional love of Christ that was
resting powerfully upon me. I wept for hours. Even in the days
that followed this experience when I would be out in the in
the market or I would be at work, when the memory of this
experience would come into my mind I would begin to weep
uncontrollable because I would feel the same unconditional
love of Jesus Christ wash over me in waves and billows.

Jesus loves each of us unconditionally. There aren't enough
words in any human language that would allow me to articu-
late the depth and the height of the love that Jesus has for you.

I began to wonder about this, and I began to seek God all the
more. What did it mean to have angels assigned to me? More-
over, this testimony, my friends, was the beginning of angelic
ministry in my life. At this point the Lord began to show me
that we do have the liberty to co-labor with His angels. Over
the process of time the Lord began to show me how this is possible. Over the course of over a decade He has given me many
more experiences like the one outlined in this chapter. The
Lord has also given me what I call Kingdom Keys to help others
activate the eyes of their understanding to see and hear from
the heavenly realms. In fact, Jesus called me to teach about this
aspect of His Kingdom in Kansas City in 2007. In the following
chapter we will begin to look at other testimonies of angelic
encounters and start to learn scriptural principles about this
aspect of Christ's Kingdom.

## CHAPTER 2

# Jesus Releases the First Angel

A few days after this first experience, I was once again in my prayer closet and I was praying and interceding. I was asking the Lord to reveal His Kingdom to me. I was asking the Lord for the opportunity to meet the King of Glory Face-to-face like that guy Saul in Acts 9. I should also mention that I was also fasting a lot. You see, I have read in the scriptures where this Man named Jesus had fasted. So, I thought to myself: "If it was good enough for Jesus, then it should also be good for me." I was asking God, "Lord, what does it mean to have four angels assigned to me?" Suddenly I had a second vision of Jesus. (You have to understand that I had only been born again for a few weeks; I simply believed that because I had read about these things in the Bible, it was normal for Christians to have these types of experiences.) When I saw Jesus in this second vision, I was very excited because Jesus was motioning with His arms for me to come to Him again. I desperately wanted to be back in the presence of Jesus. So immediately I acquiesced and said, "Yes, Lord, I want to come to You."

At that instant I felt the same sensation as before; it felt like my spirit was being vacuumed out of my body and for about two minutes I felt the sensation of ascending up through the heavens. Once again I came into the same place and fell to my knees in the very presence of Jesus. The love and compassion of Christ washed over me in waves and in billows, and once again I began to weep violently because of the love that Jesus Christ carries within His heart for me.

Again, two of the angels with Him moved forward and helped me to stand. I began to study these angels. Over the years I have seen these angels at different times, in different places, in different cities, and in different nations. One angel has beautiful blonde hair; another has shoulder-length sandy brown hair. All of them seemed to be dressed in immaculate white robes. These robes seemed to be phosphorescent; they emanate translucent rainbow colors when they move.

The two angels helped me to stand. Once again the Lord Jesus came over to me and looked deeply into my eyes. The eyes of Jesus Christ are so beautiful, so very beautiful! They are full of love and compassion. Once again the waves of God's love began to wash over me. And once again, I was undone from being in the very presence of Jesus. The Lord smiled at me. After a few moments passed, He indicated to one of the angels to come forward. Jesus said, "Kevin, today I'm assigning this angel to your ministry." The Lord Jesus told me what this angel's name was. He also told me that this angel was assigned to help release provision and also protection.

The Lord showed me that when I was instructed to release, loose, or activate this angel, he would work upon my behalf or *for* the benefit of others to bring supernatural provision or protection into people's lives.

Again, my mind began to race as I wondered what it meant to have an angel assigned to me. This angel looked at me. He has beautiful blue eyes and immaculate teeth. He was wearing a white robe with a beautiful blue sash. And he had a sword in a sheath upon his waist. He smiled at me with reassurance. And then I looked back into the eyes of Jesus. The Lord began to explain to me how I would know the time would be right to utilize this angel.

In my mind I was wondering what it meant to have an angel assigned to me. I found myself in a mental quandary. I had no grid for this type of mindset. However, the Lord is so gracious that He gives us revelation in increments that we can absorb and handle. This was a supernatural mindset. This was certainly a Kingdom mindset, and the Lord was about the business of shattering my old way of thinking and creating in me the mind of Christ (1 Corinthians 2:16). My mind was filled with questions! It seemed that thousands of thoughts and doubts just flooded into my mind and these unholy ideas sought to dissuade me from pressing into this aspect of Christ's Kingdom. But I knew that these angels of God were real, and I was certain that God's angels were ministering *for* me! I wanted to ask Jesus so many things. But almost as quickly as it began, this experience was over. And once again I found myself back in my prayer closet—weeping, weeping, weeping, and wondering what it meant to have an angel assigned to me and wondering how in the world I could work with God's angels. Over the last dozen years or so I have been given further revelation and understanding of how we can actually work with God's angels.

God's angels are released or activated by the word of the Father. The precious Holy Spirit plays an important role in activating God's angels to work with (or work *for*) or to co-labor with us. As we pray in the name of Jesus Christ, the Father releases His angels to help us or to minister *for* us (Psalm 103:20). Hebrews 1:13-14 outlines this Kingdom principle regarding God's angelic hosts very clearly:

> *But to which of the angels has He ever said: "Sit at My right hand, Till I make Your enemies Your footstool"? Are they not all ministering spirits* [angels] *sent forth to minister for those who will inherit salvation?*

Note how this scripture denotes that God's angels minister *for* you and not to you. This is a huge difference. The Lord sends His angels to take an active role in our lives. The Holy Spirit breathed upon this scripture as I fasted and prayed about why and how Jesus had assigned angels to me. The Lord's angels work for us, or co-labor with us, to further the Kingdom of God and the King of Glory. Really it is quite simple. The other remarkable thing about this scriptural principle about God's angels is that you never have to actually see God's angels to work or co-labor with them. That should take a lot of pressure off many of you reading this. This spiritual principle about God's angels is spelled out in Psalm 103:20:

> *Bless the LORD, you His angels, Who excel in strength, who do His word, Heeding the voice of His word.*

You see, as we decree (speak out loud) the Bible, the canon of Scripture, over our lives, God's angels heed the word of God and work to perform it in our lives and in our sphere of influence. This revelation helped to spark an incredibly fast and supernatural transformation in my life and circumstances as I spoke and decreed God's promises from His word over my unfortunate circumstances during this period of my life. In fact, you can also spark a God-ordained transformation in your life too as you release God's angels in your sphere of influence by speaking the word of God audibly over your circumstances and your current situation too. One method you can use to help you develop your ability to declare God's life changing scriptures can be found in the little book *"31 Word Decrees That Can Revolutionize Your Life".* Use it liberally every day. Of course, the Holy Spirit can also help you to develop your own individual "life post" scriptures to speak over your life and current circumstances too. By declaring God's word over your life you will be activating God's angels to co-labor with you and to work *for* you to transform your life (Psalm 103:20). You can move from poverty to prosperity, from sickness to health, from hopelessness to hope, and from darkness into God's marvelous light!

CHAPTER 3

# Entertaining Angels

In November 2001 the Lord opened a door for me to travel to Canada. While I was there Jesus visited me and released a supernatural impartation to me that activated me and enabled me to see and discern God's angels that were working all around me and with me. (Later I will be elaborating more on the four angels who Jesus had assigned to me in the heavenly places as this happened before this trip to the Great White North.) I want you to understand that at times we will see angels in the heavenly realms but at other times angels will appear to us in the earthly realms. In a little while I will share several testimonies from a time I was in Canada when God began to open up my spiritual eyes to see angels in the natural, in the terrestrial, and in the earthly realm. Those kinds of angelic encounters are referred to as "open eyed" visions by a lot of theologians. But now I want to go forward in time a bit.

When I came back from Canada, I was hungry to see angels in America. I had just experienced an amazing season and period of about two weeks where I had seen God's angels regularly during the time I was in Canada. By the grace of God,

I saw angels almost constantly through open eyed visions. In other words, I saw God's angels in the natural realm all around me as I went about my business. Once I returned to my little house in America, my eyes were no longer open to see into the spirit to the degree that I experienced before, and I wasn't seeing angels like I had seen them in Canada. But I wanted to! It seemed to me that the heavens were brass over my head.

I could sense and discern angelic activity around me, however I wanted to actually see God's angels that were working around and ministering around me. Because of the amazing open eyed visitations and the grace that the Lord had placed upon my life to see His angels in Canada, this inability to see angels began to become frustrating for me.

I was reading my Bible; and I saw in the Book of Hebrews, chapter 13, verse 2, that many people have entertained angels without being aware of it. So in my mind I thought, "Well, if you can entertain angels and not be aware of it, I can entertain angels on purpose!" So that was my desire. I decided right then and there that I would begin to entertain God's angels. I would fast and pray and read God's word and meditate upon the times in the Scriptures where people had encounters with angels. I entertained angels in my little house for weeks before anything happened to any great degree. Kathy and I still entertain God's angels even to this day! It's fun and there is never a dull moment! I think that is one reason that there is so much angelic activity in our ministry meetings. We can welcome and recognize God's angels as they are working in our midst. When we do acknowledge them, God's angels become much more active. When we release them to minister amazing miracles, signs and wonders manifest.

It took some time, but soon I began to have manifestations of a supernatural nature in my little house. I would hear laughter and voices, and I could hear things moving around in my kitchen. So I simply began to entertain the angels. I would say, "Hey guys, if you're hungry get yourself something to eat. There's some Kool-Aid in the refrigerator. There are ramen noodles. You know, just make yourself at home. Whatever you want, just help yourself." Looking back on it now, it's kind of silly because I don't think angels really like Kool-Aid; but, you know, I was entertaining them.

This went on for perhaps several weeks. As I entertained the angels, the amount of supernatural activity in the house began to escalate. I began to hear the angels more frequently and just had a "knowing" that angels were present. And really, this is the unction of the Holy Spirit. First John says that we have an unction of the Holy One and we know all things (2:20, KJV). So I began to have a knowing that angels were in my house. In this fashion I developed my spiritual senses by reason of use over time (Hebrews 5:14). This is also a type of spiritual discernment. You can exercise your spiritual senses in this way too.

Not long after this I was in my prayer room praying again when I began to hear noises and laughter in my living room in my little house at Beech Street. I thought, "It really sounds like there are people out there in my living room." The voices were so loud that they were interrupting my train of thought as I was seeking to pray and ask God to allow me to see and discern His angels. So I jumped up from the floor where I had been lying and praying and waiting upon God. I walked out of the bathroom door very quietly and quickly walked into the living room. And when I did, I saw angels!

Sitting there in my old worn-out couch on Beech Street was the large angel who Jesus had assigned to me in the realms of heaven! He looked up at me and seemed to be as surprised to see me as I was to see him. But he wasn't alone. All around him were several other smaller angels. These angels appeared to be adolescents. There were about seven of them, and they all appeared to be young men. They all had blonde hair, and they all had light colored eyes; most of them had beautiful blue eyes. I think a couple of the angels had light blue or green eyes.

When I walked in there, they had been laughing and actually it seemed like they had been playing around and wrestling with one another. It seemed to me that they were causing a ruckus and that is what alerted me to their presence! They were having fun! Then they all froze in place for just a moment. The angels were perfectly still as if seeking to hide from me, kind of like a deer would stand still to avoid being seen. So when they saw me step through the doorway and look at them, they were surprised. The angels were astonished because they realized I could see them. For a moment there was a pregnant pause as the seven angels looked at me and the large angel looked at me and I looked at them. We all glanced back and forth at one another for several seconds. It was a supernatural stare down for a moment!

After about thirty seconds, the young angels looked to the larger angel who was now standing in front of the couch. He had his beautiful white wings stretched out. It seemed that he had been fluttering his wings over the younger angels. When they looked at him, he laughed and smiled and he looked at me. I looked back at the younger angels and they all laughed and smiled. And then I began to laugh! And so we were all laughing there in the living room. I could see them all and they were all looking at me and I was looking at them and we were all laughing! It was quite a scene; I never expected to discover a group of angels goofing around in the little house! I threw my hands up into the air and said, "Whatever!"

And when I blinked my eyes and opened them again, I could no longer see my angelic visitors but I could still hear them. The young ones snickered! They laughed and carried on. I said, "You know what, guys? You just help yourself. You're welcome here. Make yourself at home. Get yourself something to eat. You are welcome here as long as you want to stay." And I turned around and went back into my little prayer room and began to thank the Lord Jesus Christ that He had opened up my spiritual eyes again to see His angelic host in America.

And that's the testimony about how I first began to entertain angels. My friends, you can entertain God's angels too. Jesus said that if you, being evil, know how to give your children good gifts, how much more will your Father in heaven give you the Holy Spirit (Luke 11:13). I believe that our Father in heaven is able to give us very good gifts. When we ask Him for the hidden treasures of His Kingdom, He'll give them to us. The Bible says in the Book of Psalms that God will give us the desires of our heart (37:4). If the desire of your heart is to see God's angels, He will open your eyes to see them. In Ephesians, chapter 3, the word of God says that He will do exceedingly abundantly above all that we could think, ask, or imagine (v. 20). So if you ask God to see angels, He will do exceedingly above anything you can imagine. And remember, Jesus Himself said, *"Whatever you ask anything in My name, that I will do, that the Father may be glorified"* (John 14:13 ). So, my friends; when we ask God to be aware of His Kingdom and to see His angels, He can easily open our eyes (spiritual vision) and allow us to see them. That is what I believe!

# Entertaining Angels
# in Moravian Falls

At the Mount of Transfiguration, Jesus chose to take three of His disciples to a specific geographic location at a fixed or appointed time. There God poured out a supernatural grace to activate the seer anointing in the lives of Peter, James, and John. We see this in Matthew 17:1-2:

> *Now after six days* [a specific time] *Jesus took Peter, James, and John his brother, led them up on a high mountain* [a specific place] *by themselves; and He was transfigured before them.*

Again, these are important keys to opening the heavens over your life. The disciples entered into the spirit by proximity, by practicing chronological and geographical obedience.

In 2006 Kathy and I were living in Kansas City, Missouri. We were experiencing wonderful supernatural encounters, angelic visitations, and great grace upon our lives and the ministry in Kansas City. In 2002, the Lord had spoken to me in a mud hut in Murchison Falls, Uganda, and instructed me to move to Kansas City and to submit to the spiritual authority of the leadership at Christ Triumphant Church. In February of 2006 the Lord spoke to me very clearly again instructing us to move to Moravian Falls, North Carolina. Quite frankly, I did not want to leave Kansas City. You see, we had grace and favor there. We were members of a wonderful fellowship, Christ Triumphant Church.

It was the first time in my life that I had a pastor who loved and fully supported the ministry. And on top of all of that, our home was free and clear of any mortgage and there was a lake in my backyard that was full of bass. You see, I love to bass fish. Sometimes the Holy Spirit goes fishing with me and tells me where to cast my line. In fact, there are even places in heaven where you can fish and swim in the rivers of God. (If you would like to read more testimonies about all of the beautiful places in heaven and what they look like, get my book *Angels in the Realms of Heaven*.)

## "Supernatural"

Nonetheless, in obedience to the Lord, I simply told the Him, "OK, Lord; we will move, just tell us when." The Lord instructed us to prepare our home to sell and to move in 2008. Now I hope that this testimony will be encouraging to many of you who the Lord is nudging to move geographically. I call this geographical obedience. When we put our home on the market at the exact time that Lord had told us to, we received an offer to buy it even before the For Sale sign was placed in the yard! Can you say *"supernatural"*?

When we moved to Moravian Falls, the Lord instructed me to take a one-year sabbatical and to focus on building our little log cabin. He told me not to do any ministry—zero! I have to admit, it was a stretch for me and many were the late nights that I wondered if I had missed the Lord by making the move to Moravian Falls. I had promised Kathy that we would move into the new log cabin by November 27th of 2008, Thanksgiving. So I was working hard to meet that goal.

*Sometimes when you are seeking to be chronologically and geographically obedient the Lord will test you.*

One October night I had determined to work late. It had been a rough day. I had smashed my finger and it was throbbing; I also cut this same finger and it was bleeding on and off. The day was unusually warm, and I was sweating profusely. That day I literally poured blood, sweat, and tears into our little cabin! Kathy was visiting our family in another state. So, I decided to work as late as I could stand it in an effort to meet the deadline. I was sawing and putting up trim. I was not feeling particularly "*spiritual*" that night. I worked up until about 1:30 a.m. I accidently hit my bleeding and throbbing finger again, so I decided to call it a night.

I did not want to lose the hour and a half it would take me to drive back and forth between the cabin and the house we were renting, so I had gone to a local discount store and picked up a cheap cot and a little blanket. I pulled the temporary power and cut off all of the electricity. I took my little flashlight and my cot and settled in one of the unfinished bedrooms on the second floor. It was littered with sheetrock dust and my sweat and blood!

I took my travel Bible out and began to read the word by flashlight. I looked at the time and it was now past 2:30 a.m. (Psalm 23). I was totally exhausted. As I drifted off to sleep, I asked the Lord if I had missed Him by moving to Moravian Falls and building this cabin. I was not doing any ministry; and to top things off, my hands hurt, I was covered in blood, and I smelled of sweat. I thought, "Could this really be God?" This thought took the form of a *"heart prayer."*

About 4 a.m. I was startled into consciousness! Confused for a moment, I wondered if my little "heart prayer," asking the Lord if I had missed Him with the move to North Carolina, had continued; perhaps I was praying in my sleep. I awoke to discover that the manifest glory of God was suspended in the room; the reverential fear of the Lord was also hovering in that unfinished, second floor bedroom! When I opened my eyes, I saw a very bright white phosphorescent supernatural light was illuminating the room. There was no electricity, and my little flashlight was lying on the floor beside me, off. Every hair on my body seemed to stand on end, and I wondered if it were possible to crawl under the floorboards.

## Parchment and Leather

Suddenly I saw a large eight-foot tall angel appear at the foot of my cot! It was the glory and glow that was coming from this angelic being that was lighting up the room. I was frozen by the angel's proximity. He was dressed in what looked to be a colonial style jacket with a big brass belt buckle and big brass buttons. This angelic being was also wearing a big hat that was adorned with a large brass looking buckle in the front. He had great big bushy eyebrows; one eyebrow was raised up at a sharp angle as he stared intently at me. In his big calloused hands was a large ledger or book of some sort. It looked to be ancient, and I thought that I could smell parchment and leather exuding from the angel's book.

This angelic messenger was glancing back and forth between the book and me with a perplexed and somewhat menacing countenance. The pages of his book were flipping by very fast like the wings of a hummingbird. I lay there for what seemed like an eternity, stunned by the presence and glory of this angelic visitor. After a few minutes the angel took his right index finger and jammed it into the book, which stopped the pages from flipping by. The angel glanced at me again, and then I watched him scan the writing as he moved his finger down the page. After a short while he stopped and looked up at me with a twinkle in his bright green eyes.

He looked at me a little more intently, as if he were trying to recognize me. I watched as his pupils focused. At that moment a welcoming smile creased his lips and his stern expression seemed to melt into acceptance. As the smile spread across his face, he said in a booming voice, "You are welcome here!" I did not recognize the accent that the angel spoke with. I lay there frozen by the fear of Lord and by the presence of my supernatural visitor. My eyes were now glued to the angel standing at the foot of my little cot.

I examined him carefully for about ten more seconds. His big green eyes locked with mine for an instant. A twinkle flashed in his eyes. My angelic visitor smiled at me once more, nodded his head slightly in my direction, and suddenly he vanished, leaving the glory and reverential fear of God lingering in the unfinished bedroom. After the angel had been gone for a while and the fear of the Lord subsided a little, I began to wonder if I should have asked my angelic visitor some questions. As I pondered these things in my heart, the supernatural light continued to illuminate the room for several more moments after the angel's abrupt departure. Eventually the light of the glory faded. However, I found that I was still frozen by fear in the darkness. The odor of my perspiration was now mingled with a wonderful heavenly fragrance of parchment, leather, lavender, and roses.

## "Heart Prayer"

Some our friends who have stayed in that bedroom in our log home have experienced angelic encounters. I believe that the heavens were ripped open there when this angelic messenger, whom I believe to be a Moravian, stepped into the room on that warm October night. Since that time I have had literally dozens of angelic visitations in our log home in Moravian Falls. I must admit, it was nice to know that we were welcomed in the "*spirit.*" I have occasionally wondered what would have happened to someone who was *not* "welcome here."

Perhaps the Lord released this angel as an answer to my "*heart prayer.*" Remember, prayer is one of the two most important keys to opening the heavens over your life. Perhaps the Lord sent this messenger to give me revelation of the fact that God *had* positioned me in a "certain" place where the heavens were open to a greater degree. Perhaps this was the fruit of our chronological and geographical obedience. I certainly know that God releases angels and opens the heavens over peoples' lives in Moravian Falls. I could share many testimonies along this line.

On February 25, 2009, the Lord visited me at our little log home and assigned a "scribe" angel to me. Since that time I have written many books including the trilogy on angels and others with the help of this "scribe" angel. Again, this is another mysterious and glorious aspect of the Kingdom of Heaven and another of the hidden mysteries of the seer anointing. Surely God is unlocking these hidden mysteries of His Kingdom and giving them to His friends at this hour. Supernatural encounters like the one I just shared may become more and more common for you. It is possible that when you activate your seer gifting and learn to walk in the seer anointing with maturity and wisdom you will also begin to see and discern God's angelic beings.

## Obedient to the Spirit

The ability to discern angels can manifest in various ways. The activation or impartation of the gifts of the spirit and the seer anointing is often the fruit or outcome that unfolds in a person's life when they enter into or experience an open heaven. The last testimony shares a modern day example of this dynamic of the seer anointing activating during a supernatural experience or open heaven encounter.

Perhaps the Lord will use a similar pattern in your life. Sometimes people cannot experience open heavens and get the seer anointing and all of the associated blessings activated in their lives because they are geographically disobedient. One of my neighbors says it this way, "*If you are not in the place that God has called you to be, you will find that there is no grace to be in the place where you are.*" I like to say that we need grace for our place! By the way, through a supernatural series of events and the grace of God we were able to finished building our log home and received our certificate of occupancy on November 17th of 2008. We enjoyed a great turkey dinner the first Thanksgiving under the open heavens in our little log home.

So allow me to encourage you to be obedient to the leadings of the Holy Spirit when you are asked to travel to a new place. Perhaps the Lord has a purpose for such a trip, and it could be something that God requires of you. Your obedience to take such a trip could turn out to be your Mount of Transfiguration experience. I call these prophetic acts of obedience. Search for places or geographic areas that are under an open heaven, and invest time seeking the Lord there. Jerusalem is a great example of a geographic place like this. I have had numerous angelic encounters in the Holy City. In 2011 a fiery angel visited Kathy and I in the Ramada Inn in Jerusalem!

A geographic place where the heavens are opened can be called a Mahanaim. There are lots of places like this on the earth today. Again, I call this chronological and geographical obedience. These are two very important keys to unlocking your ability to see and discern God's angels as they are working in and around your life.

## CHAPTER 5

# The Mighty Worship Angel

In 2001 and 2002 that God began to ask me to do some unusual things. Some people call these acts of prophetic obedience. God spoke to me to travel to Springdale, Newfoundland, Canada, in November. And it is really cold in Canada in November, especially in Newfoundland. I had been getting beaten up in the church, and in my mind I had purposed to go to St. John in the Virgin Islands. I thought it would be nice; just me and Jesus snorkeling with the fish. I just wanted to get away from the "bully pulpit." But the Lord began to instruct me to go to Newfoundland. I didn't realize it at that time but there is a St. John's in Newfoundland.

The Lord had instructed me to begin to pray in the Holy Spirit on my trip to Newfoundland. I began to pray in another language; I began to pray in the Spirit. I prayed all the way from West Virginia to Virginia to the airport in Roanoke, Virginia. Then I prayed in the Spirit from Roanoke, Virginia, to Washington, DC. Then from Washington, DC, to Halifax, Nova Scotia, I prayed in the Spirit. Then from Nova Scotia I prayed in the Holy Spirit all the way to Newfoundland. For about eighteen or twenty hours, I prayed constantly in the Holy Ghost. And I believe that is another supernatural key that can unlock the realms of the supernatural in your life. Jude 1:20 says to build yourself up by praying in the Holy Spirit. Praying in the Spirit is an important key that can activate your ability to see and discern angelic activity.

When I arrived in Springdale, God began to open my spiritual eyes. I had several encounters where I began to feel angels touching my body, touching my hands. We were preparing for a set of revival meetings at a small church called Living Waters Ministries in the little city of Springdale, Newfoundland, Canada. As time passed my ability to discern angels increased.

On the first night of those meetings, I was near the front row worshiping God with all of my heart. And I felt the power and glory of Jesus come into the service. It felt very similar to what I had experienced when Jesus had invited me to come into the realms of heaven. The glory of God began to wash over me in wave after wave as there I stood with my hands raised in the air worshiping Jesus in the spirit and in truth (John 4:24). I felt the glory of God fall upon me like a mighty tidal wave, and I was instantly inundated with the love of God.

I opened my eyes and I looked at the worship team; there were about five musicians on the worship team. But I noticed behind the worship team—behind two of the women, Rose and Coleen—there was an unusually tall man. In my mind I thought, "I don't remember him being there before." I looked more intently at him and realized that he was very tall, about nine and a half feet tall. As I continued to look at him, he turned and looked at me with a stern look; and then he smiled at me.

I also noticed that he was dressed unusually; he was wearing a white robe and he had golden sandals on his feet.

It suddenly occurred to me that I was seeing one of God's angels. This mesmerized me. I was overwhelmed by the glory that I felt, but I continued to stare at this angel, thinking perhaps I was seeing something that wasn't there. So I shook my head and closed my eyes and entered again into the midst of worship. But when I opened my eyes, this angel was still there! He was smiling at me; and not only did he smile at me, he winked one of his eyes as if to say, "Hello!" I continued to look at every aspect of this angel. God allowed me to see this angel for the duration of the service; I estimate for over an hour.

He was a good nine and a half feet tall with long, curly, light brown hair and piercing blue eyes. He had an immaculate smile; his teeth were perfect. His robe seemed to radiate the glory of God. It was phosphorescent; it looked as if every color in the rainbow would shimmer from his robe as he would move slightly. Upon his waist he had a wide belt; attached to it were several articles, including a large sword which he had sheathed. This angel stood with his arms crossed across his powerful chest. He looked powerful. He continued to look at me from time to time and would smile at me. Somehow I understood that he was a mighty warrior angel that was there on assignment.

On another note; even as I am writing this in my office at the (iMAEC) International Ministry Apostolic Equipping Center here in Moravian Falls, North Carolina, there are beautiful angel feathers that are swirling around my head. I know by the Spirit that God's angels really get excited when we recognize them and when we write about their exploits. Perhaps the reason for this is that God's angels will have no other testimony when they stand before the Lord except the testimonies of the times that they have co-labored with us (humans) to help further the Kingdom of Heaven. Just a thought that I sensed you might like to know. Now back to the testimony at hand. I love it when these minute and tiny little white angels' feathers manifest. They are little supernatural kisses from heaven!

Somehow I knew this angel had been sent there to break open the heavens; and some way he would have an influence on what would take place in the meetings. I watched as this angel looked at different people in the church. Somehow I knew that he was able to look into their hearts, that this heavenly visitor knew the things hidden deep within each of our hearts. As time passed I was mesmerized by the sight. He was powerful, he was a warrior, and he had been sent ahead with a specific assignment for those meetings in that church and to help release the Kingdom of Heaven in Springdale. When the service was ending, I watched as this angel ascended back up into the heavens.

I was totally undone by the things that I had seen. Later I realized that this was just the beginning of what God was going to open up to me and allow me to see and discern, not only in Canada but many other places in the future. This understanding has proven to be totally true and accurate as I have seen angels in almost every nation that I have traveled to preach the Gospel of the Kingdom. If you are counting, that is thirty-eight nations as of this writing. I give Him praise!

My friends, God wants you to see these things too. God wants everyone to be aware of His angelic host. They are around us at all times. Some angels have specific assignments. I believe each of us has at least one angel who is assigned to protect us. Jesus said in the Book of Matthew that children's angels always behold the face of their Father (18:10). Do you think just because you grow up to be an adult that you lose your angel? No, I believe God has assigned an angel to you and that angel is with you for the duration of your time upon earth. So it is possible for you to co-labor with the angels who God has assigned to you.

## CHAPTER 6

# A Band of Angels

As I said in the last testimony, God had opened up my spiritual eyes to see this mighty angel during the worship service. When that happened, God began to activate my ability to see into the spirit or spiritual dimensions. Today I call this the seer anointing. Later in 2002 Jesus spoke to me about the "seers of old." During these revival meetings in the little city of Springdale, Newfoundland, Canada, God began to open up my spiritual eyes to see into the spirit beyond anything that I could have ever hoped for or imagined.

At one point I saw a stream of golden oil flowing into the church from a small hole that seemed to be spinning above the ceiling of the church. I knelt upon the spot where I saw that golden oil, and the power and anointing of the Holy Spirit filled me. I fell upon the carpet. As I lay there, this golden oil poured out upon me. During that time I could feel angels dancing around me and brushing their wings across my face. I found this to be totally normal for some reason.

Over the next few days, I continued to see that little opening spinning in the sanctuary. And it seemed as if when we worshiped Jesus, the opening began to bloom. I guess you could call it a portal. I watched over the course of several days as that portal went from the size of a fifty-cent piece to a foot in circumference, then two feet in circumference, and then four feet in circumference.

During this time, during the worship times, many people in the church began to tell one another about how they were hearing angels singing along with the worship team. And they were hearing instruments that didn't belong to the setting; instruments that were other worldly were being heard by many people in the church. And I was hearing them too.

On the first night of these meetings, I was lying upon the floor and I watched this portal begin to enlarge. And to my astonishment, I began to see small angels come up to the edge of the portal. By now this opening in the heavens was about twenty-five to forty feet in circumference. These angels looked like toddlers, and they had little musical instruments that were fashioned to fit their little chubby hands. They had little wings and they had little instruments that seemed to be like xylophones or harps or woodwind instruments. As the worship team praised Jesus, the little angels entered in and worshiped Jesus too. They were chubby little things; and they played their instruments with zeal and they sang with the most beautiful voices, worshiping the Lamb of God. They joined right in with the worship team at Living Waters Church. This new development astonished me! It was quite amazing to observe this little band of angels as they were poking fun at me. They were whispering to one another, and pointing at me and laughing. They were really having a good ole time! In fact, so was I!

I lay upon the floor and I watched them for the entire worship service. After several minutes one of the little angels nudged the angel to his right with his elbow and pointed down at me. It was similar to the time when the angels in my little house at Beech Street were surprised that I could see them. This little angel pointed down and he told the others something in a language I didn't understand.

I could hear the words but I couldn't understand their language because they were speaking a language that was foreign to me. The Bible talks about angels having their own language or "tongue" (1 Corinthians 13:1).

The angels began to laugh and giggle at me because they realized I could see them. I couldn't move, unfortunately, or I would have waved at them. I believe that these little angels knew that I was not able to move and perhaps that was the reason for their amusement? But I lay there and I watched them as they giggled and played around. I watched them as they played their percussion instruments and their woodwind instruments and their stringed instruments. After a few moments all the angels realized I could see them, but they just continued to worship Jesus and every now and then they would nod at me or wink at me or smile at me. I would nod or smile back; I wish I could have waved but I was unable to move my hands. You see, I was under a weighty, powerful glory and anointing of the Holy Spirit. It seemed that I was glued to the floor!

Over the course of three days, I saw these angels numerous times. I really can't tell you what kind of angels they were, but I can tell you that they loved to adore and worship the Lamb of God. My friends, when you are in a worship setting and you are worshiping Jesus with all of your heart, it is a beautiful opportune time to exercise your spiritual senses according to the principle of Hebrews 5:14. It is a great time to perceive the angelic activity that goes on in worship. I believe God wants you and me to understand that His angels were created to worship Jesus. I have seen and know that there is an incredible variety of angelic beings that inhabit the heavenly realm. Jesus has angels of every shape and size that you could imagine, and not all of them look like humans! In the next chapter I will describe one such angelic being.

## CHAPTER 7

# My Encounter with a Seraph

During this time when I was in Newfoundland, Canada, I pur-posed in my heart to travel to several of these revival meetings that were taking place in different cities. We traveled to the city of St. John's because I was hungry for more of Jesus. When we arrived at the service, I could hear angels singing. I could hear their instruments but I was not able to see the angels with my eyes. I was a bit disappointed, although it was nice to hear them and it was nice to discern that there were angels nearby. But I was quite disappointed that I couldn't see them. I was only able to discern a similitude of them.

During the ministry I once again found myself lying in a horizontal position on the floor, unable to move. I was once more under the power and glory of the Holy Spirit and glued to the floor. I began to hear a loud sound; the only way I could describe the sound is similar to a helicopter. As I was lying on the floor unable to move, I began to see something zipping back and forth in the sanctuary with my peripheral vision. I focused my eyes, and what I saw truly astonished me. I saw what appeared to be a hummingbird the size of a human being. This hummingbird's wings were moving supernaturally fast. As it moved and as its wings fluttered by, it was like phosphorescent colors were cast off in every direction from this creature's wings. And I realized that it was an angel. But I'd never seen an angel like that; I had no idea what it was. Now that I look back on it a decade later, I believe I had an encounter with a seraph.

I watched this angel as it moved through the sanctuary for about twenty minutes. I was astonished. I never could actually see its face, although from time to time I would see a profile of its face. It might look like a lion or some other animal; but I could never focus because it moved so swiftly all I could see were waves of color coming from its wings. After a while I was astounded as this angel came directly at me in a straight line. And when it did I could hear the sound of its wings fluttering very, very fast. Its wings were moving supernaturally fast and it seemed that they spun around in all directions simultaneously. It was truly remarkable to see such a creature up close and personal like this! What an amazing God that we serve who creates such diverse and wondrous spiritual beings such as this!

I could smell frankincense and myrrh as this angel approached me. It appeared to have something in its hands, some instrument in its hands; and in that instrument appeared to be a coal of fire about the size of a man's hand. The angel few up to me, and I saw as it took its hand and touched my lips with that burning coal of fire. The moment the angel touched me with that coal of fire, electricity and heat went into my lips and into my tongue and into my jaws. I could feel a tingling sensation as it moved through my mouth, my tongue, my jaws, my lips; and then it went into my spinal cord and went up and down my spine and up into my brain. I could feel the power of God as it moved through my brain. I felt like I was being rewired and ministered to.

I had my eyes closed because it was actually painful; it was burning. When I opened my eyes, I saw this angel remove the coal of fire from my lips; then it ascended up, moved off to the right, and disappeared. I was in pain; this fire was burning in my lips, this fire was burning in my tongue, and this fire was burning in my mind. I didn't understand what was happening. I was unable to move; I was fearful as I was sort of glued to the floor. I lay there for a long time. In fact, I lay there so long that the church service ended. Finally one of the church elders came and said, "You're going to have to leave." He helped me to get up from the floor, but I could hardly move. I could hardly walk. It seemed that I was supernaturally heavy from the glory of God that was resting upon me that evening.

One thing I noticed was that my mouth and my tongue and my lips when I articulated words seemed to function and operate differently now. Perhaps God had given me the tongue of the learned. When I began to think, my mind seemed to form thoughts differently. Perhaps God had used that angel to transform my mind. This experience shattered the paradigm I had about all of God's angels being warm and fuzzy. Many are powerful and strange!

Saints, there are hidden mysteries in the Kingdom of God. There are mysteries which are in hidden in Christ's Kingdom that we don't know about. First Corinthians, chapter 2, verses 9-11 tells us:

*It is written: "Eye has not seen, nor ear heard, Nor have entered into the heart of man The things which God has prepared for those who love Him." But God has revealed them to us through His Spirit. For the Spirit searches all things, yes, the deep things of God. For what man knows the things of a man except the spirit of the man which is in him? Even so no one knows the things of God except the Spirit of God.*

Some theologians call these mysterious things the silence of the Scriptures. I don't know for sure. But I can tell you that when I encountered Christ's seraph, my mind was renewed and I was changed. And I believe God has angels like that, that are available to minister to you too. That is if you are willing to allow one of God's fiery seraphim minister *for* you!

CHAPTER 8

# Mighty Harvester Angel— Singapore

When God began to activate me and show me how to work with His angels, it sparked a supernatural release of ministry in my life. God put into motion a metamorphosis in my life that was initiated when Jesus showed me how to implement angelic ministry in my life and within my sphere of influence. And I give Him the glory for that.

We all have angels of the Most High God that we can work with to transform our circumstances and our lives. God's angels perform God's word to minister for heirs of salvation. That's you, if you believe in Jesus Christ and He is your Messiah or Savior; if you are what the church calls "born again." I thank God for that. If you are an heir of Jesus Christ's free gift of salvation, you are prepared to work with God's angels. However, you need to understand that you may never have to actually see one of the Lord's angels to be released to work with them. "Why?" you may ask. Because God's angels obey His word; and when you believe and speak God's anointed word out over your life, His angels will work on your behalf to see that God's word comes to pass in your life (Psalm 103:20; Hebrews 1:14).

In 2006 the Lord opened up the door for my wife, Kathy, and I to travel to Singapore and minister at the Church of Our Savior. What a wonderful place and what gracious people they are! They treated us with kindness. We had been invited to minister at a healing service on Saturday evening. This was to be a bilingual service. About one-half of the people in the congregation, of several hundred people who were in attendance, did not speak English; they spoke Chinese.

As I preached the message about faith and Christ's atonement and the power of Jesus to heal us today through simple faith in His Cross and the work He did upon His Cross, I felt as if there was loss in the translation, as a young man translated my message into Chinese. So I let out a little heart's prayer that went something like this: "Lord, I don't think I'm getting through. I need Your help."

The instant this prayer went forth from my heart, I felt a wind blow into the sanctuary of the Church of Our Savior; it seemed to blow around in a circle. I felt the anointing of God come into the sanctuary. For a moment I looked to the rear of the auditorium and I saw a large angel standing there. It was the first time I had seen an angel this big. He was about forty-five to fifty feet tall. He was magnificent, he was powerful, and I knew that God had released this angel in answer to my prayer. Perhaps this was the angel of Singapore? I am not certain, but today I know and understand that there are Godly angels that are assigned to cities, states, regions, and even nations. At times God will allow His ministers to co-labor with angels that have Kingdom authority over the regions or even nations that they are working and ministering in at that time.

I saw the angel clearly for a moment and then I was no longer able to see him with my eyes; it was no longer an open vision. That only lasted for a moment. But as I preached the message of the Cross, I could see this angel for fleeting moments at a time. He was beautiful; he had long brown hair, a mighty sword was in his hand, and he had magnificent white wings. At times I was able to discern this angel's similitude. As I preached the word of God, he would flutter his wings back and forth over the congregation in the sanctuary. It seemed as if when he would move his wings back and forth, a moment or so later I could feel the wind of his wings and the glory of God as it would wash over the congregation and reach me on the platform. The angel was about an estimated one hundred and fifty feet away.

At the end of my message I gave an altar call or invitation to receive Jesus Christ as Savior. At first very few people responded; maybe five or six people stood up and came to the altar to receive Jesus Christ as Savior. I looked in the back for a fleeting moment and I saw the angel clearly. He was moving his wings more vigorously now, and the wind of his wings began to reach me at the altar. I could smell the fragrance of frankincense and I could feel the wind that was generated when he fluttered his wings over the sanctuary. I continued to encourage the people to come, telling them that Christ's salvation was free. And people began to come forward; first a few and then a few more and after a while there were dozens of people who came to receive Jesus Christ as Savior.

At the end of the message as I led the people in the prayer of salvation, I glanced at the back of the auditorium. I saw this mighty angel standing with his sword back in his sheath and his arms folded across his chest. He was mighty and powerful and strong, and for a moment he looked at me and smiled. And I knew that he was pleased with the outcome of my message. I believe that this was one of the angels that the Book of Revelation speaks about; that God would send His angels to preach the everlasting Gospel to every tongue to every tribe and to every nation (14:6). And I've often wondered if that angel I saw in Singapore is an angel who God has assigned to that nation or Singapore proper.

I'm not sure, but I believe there are angels like that with the anointing to take the everlasting Gospel to the nations throughout the whole earth. And the eyes of the Lord are just looking for someone who will co-labor with them to preach the everlasting Gospel of Jesus Christ to the ends of the earth.

I'm not sure what happened as that angel fluttered his wings and the glory of God filled the sanctuary of the Church of Our Savior, but I do know this: when the people stood up from their seats to come to the front to receive Jesus Christ as Savior, it was their own decision. Perhaps as the angel fluttered his wings, being that he had just come down from the very throne of heaven, he released the glory of God into the sanctuary. And perhaps in the presence of the glory of God, the people present in that service realized their need for salvation. Perhaps in that glory of God they realized their sinful state and that they needed Jesus.

After the service I had dinner with one of the pastors, and he told me that several of the other pastors were astonished that so many people had been born again that night. It seems that some of the people who were saved that night had been coming to the church literally for years, some of them over twenty years, but they had never prayed to receive Christ as Savior. They were astonished that my message was so simple yet that so many had responded to such a simple presentation of the salvation in Jesus Christ and prayed to receive Jesus as Messiah. As the pastor told me this, in my mind I was laughing a bit; because I realized it wasn't my eloquence, it wasn't my theological knowledge, it wasn't my ability to preach God's word, but it was an anointing; it was the glory of God that this angel released into the church. And in that glory, the people realized their need for a Savior.

Saints, God has angels like this that He wants you to co-labor with. And I believe that we have stepped into a day and an hour when anyone can co-labor with harvester angels like the one I saw in Singapore. God will begin to accelerate the release of these kinds of mighty harvester angels into the earth to help with the great last days harvest before the triumphant return of the Lord Jesus Christ. We see this outlined in Revelation 14:15:

*And another angel came out of the temple, crying with a loud voice to Him who sat on the cloud, "Thrust in Your sickle and reap, for the time has come for You to reap, for the harvest of the earth is ripe."*

Jesus also taught about these kinds of harvester angels in Matthew 13:37-42 (emphasis added):

> *[Jesus] answered and said to them: "He who sows the good seed is the Son of Man. The field is the world, the good seeds are the sons of the kingdom, but the tares are the sons of the wicked one. The enemy who sowed them is the devil,* **the harvest is the end of the age, and the reapers are the angels.** *Therefore as the tares are gathered and burned in the fire, so it will be at the end of this age.* **The Son of Man will send out His angels, and they will gather out of His kingdom all things that offend, and those who practice lawlessness, and will cast them into the furnace of fire. There will be wailing and gnashing of teeth."*

## CHAPTER 9

# The Mighty Angel—Bay Roberts

This testimony is about the mighty angel who transported me into heaven when I was visiting Bay Roberts, Newfoundland, Canada, between revival meetings. During this time I was traveling to these different revival meetings. One night we came to the place where we were going to stay. Rob and Linda had allowed a friend and me to stay at their home for the night after the meeting in St. John's. After the service we went to Tim Horton's to get some chicken noodle soup, so by the time we arrived at Rob and Linda's home, it was quite late.

When we got there we found a note that said they had been praying and the Lord had told them that they were to allow me to sleep in their master bedroom. I objected to this; but I was assured that if Rob and Linda wanted me to sleep in the master bedroom they had heard from the Lord, so I should do it. So I acquiesced and went into the master bedroom. It was a beautiful bedroom. They had a really large four-poster bed that was really nice. I was really blessed to be there. I was physically tired but I was spiritually energized. You see, this was the same night that the seraph had touched my lips with a coal of heavenly fire!

The moment I closed the door behind me, the presence of the Holy Spirit fell in the room. I began to weep because I felt the tangible love and glory of Jesus again. I began to pray and ask the Lord what His plans were for this night. Why was I here in this beautiful bedroom? The Lord told me to get my trusty old King James Bible and begin to read from Revelation 4. So I began to read Revelation 4. I was a new Christian; I didn't really understand it, I was just reading the words. Then the Holy Spirit whispered to me. He said, "Kevin, read the words out loud." So I began to read the words of Revelation 4 out loud: "*Behold, a door standing open in heaven*" (v. 1).

As I read I began to hear a loud whistling sound. It sounded kind of like the whistling of the jet engines on a plane. It was loud; and it continued to get louder and louder. As I looked up from my old King James Bible, I could see through the roof of the house. The ceiling had disappeared, and I could see millions of stars in the sky. In addition to this I was shocked to see another amazing celestial body! I saw a supernatural sight coming at me with at supersonic speed and accompanied by this loud whistling noise was a heavenly ball of fire! It appeared to be about eighteen inches in circumference. This ball of fire was plummeting from the realms of heaven straight at me! And before I could think or brace myself, it slammed into my solar plexus. It seemed like the entire fireball was instantly absorbed into the very fiber of my body and my being. Instantaneously I was launched out of my body (I should probably say my spirit was launched; whether in body or out of body I am not sure).

It felt like the same thing that happened in my little prayer closet when I was at Beech Street, but it was much more intense. I could feel my spirit being sucked up into the heavens. I looked down and I could see my body lying on my bed jerking. I could hear myself praying in the Holy Ghost, I saw my Bible fly off of my chest, and I saw my body convulsing as this ball of fire penetrated and was absorbed into my body. In the spirit I was being taken up into heaven.

This astonished me. So I looked to my left and I saw a large angel, a mighty angel, who had me by my left hand. He was taking me up into the realms of heaven. I don't know any other way to describe it except that I was flying through the heavenly realms with this mighty angel. He had long blonde hair, beautiful blue eyes, and such a gentle countenance about him. But he had a firm grip on my left hand. I thought, "Oh my goodness! What is happening?" Fear began to seep into my spirit. The moment this happened, the angel looked at me and smiled with reassurance and a peace came into me and I knew that this was God's doing. Then I realized that I had seen this angel in the presence of Jesus, so I relaxed.

I looked back down and I could see the house becoming smaller and smaller. And then I could see the city of Bay Roberts. And then I could see the island of Newfoundland growing smaller; I could see the lights, something like you might see from the space shuttle. In the distance I could see North America; I could see the lights of Boston and other cities. I looked the other direction and I could see the Atlantic Ocean, as I continued to accelerate higher into the heavenly realms.

After a moment or two this angel brought me to a very broad and beautiful place, and I guess you could say I "landed" on what appeared to be a beach. When I fell to my knees, I felt the power and the glory of God. I felt the same unconditional love of Jesus I had felt the first time He had called me to Him in prayer. And my knees hit the sand and I began to weep.

When I got myself together and was able to stop weeping a little bit, I began to look at my surroundings. When I looked up, there was Jesus. He appeared to be expecting me. And there behind Him were the same four angels I had seen with Him the first time I had gone to Him in prayer. These were the same four angels who Jesus had told me He was assigning to my ministry. And, once again, two of the angels came to me and helped me to stand. One angel had already been assigned to me; I knew who he was. I looked at him, he smiled, and we began to exchange greetings.

The Lord walked up to me and said, "Kevin, I've brought you here to show you some things about your future." And I began to walk with Jesus. The four angels stayed behind, but Jesus took me by the hand and we began to walk upon this beach. As we walked I was looking around at my surroundings. I could hear the sounds of harps and ethereal singing; it seemed to envelope the Lamb of God. It seemed to go with Him wherever He walked. We walked upon this sandy beach, this beautiful white sandy beach. Jesus had no sandals on; He had no shoes on, nor did I. In fact, I was dressed in a white robe. I was astonished! I saw the Lord's feet as He made footprints in the sand, and I also noticed the faint indentions of the places where the nails had pierced His feet.

I looked at the ocean and it seemed to go on forever. There was a beautiful light that emanated in this place. It wasn't like sunshine but it was a beautiful light. This ocean was perfectly still. It looked like a mirror, and it reflected the phosphorescent colors seeming to just illuminate the sky. It may have been the sea of glass like crystal; I don't know. But I do know that this began at about 1:45 a.m. and I walked with Jesus for several hours. I was with Jesus the entire night walking and talking in the heavenly places. It was paradise.

As I walked with Jesus, He began to tell me things. He began to tell me things about my future. He began to tell me things He had called me to do. And I began to get supernatural revelation that I was a new creation; old things had passed away and all things had become new (2 Corinthians 5:17). And as I walked with Jesus, He held my hand and I felt the same compassion and the same unconditional love that I had felt the first time that Jesus called me to Him.

And I knew that heaven was real and that it will be my home one day. And, my friend, if you know Jesus Christ as your Savior, it will be your home too. God has a place prepared for you in the heavenly realms; it's your inheritance. If you are not sure if you will go to heaven when you die, you can pray the prayer of salvation in the back of this book right now to be sure. Jesus and I walked and we talked about many things. It wouldn't be proper for me to share those with you in this testimony because those are pearls that I treasure and hide away in my heart.

After several hours Jesus and I returned to the spot where the mighty angel had dropped me off. And it appeared that the four angels who I had seen at the beginning of our walk were waiting for the Messiah to return. Jesus put His hands upon my shoulders and He gave me instructions as we departed.

Then instantly the same strong angel grabbed me by my left hand, and I was launched back into the spirit. I could see myself flying through time and through space. And I looked again and I saw this mighty angel who had taken me into the realms of heaven and who was now delivering me back into the realms of earth. I saw the earth come into view. I saw the continent of Europe; I saw the lights in England and Scandinavia off to my right. Somehow I knew through the unction of the Holy Spirit that it wouldn't be long until I would be in those places preaching the Gospel of Jesus Christ. (And it happened! In less than two years I was preaching and teaching in Europe and in Holland and in Sweden.)

And as this angel took me back to the realms of earth, I saw the island of Newfoundland come up. I saw the lights of the city, and then I saw Bay Roberts, and I saw the roof of Rob and Linda's house, and I saw myself lying on the bed praying in tongues. I looked once more at this angel and he smiled at me with assurance. And then instantly I was back in my body. Sweat had pooled on the bed.

I looked at the clock and realized I had been in the spirit for about six and a half hours. Although six and a half hours had passed in the natural realm, in the spirit it seemed that I was in the heavenly realms with Jesus for days. Time as we know it does not exist in heaven. There is only eternity! It is glorious!

My friend, God has angels like this with whom you can be transformed and translated and taken into heavenly places.

The testimony of Jesus is the Spirit of prophecy. I believe there can be a time in your life when you've been praying and, seeking God with all of your heart, and you can read Revelation 4 and the heavens could open up over your life. And a mighty angel could take you into the very presence of Jesus. After all, God has promised you that He would *"do exceedingly abundantly above all that we ask or think, according to the power that works in us, to Him be glory in the church by Christ Jesus to all generations, forever and ever"* (Ephesians 3:20-21).

## CHAPTER 10

# The Mighty Angel and the Weeping Room

This testimony is about the mighty angel who transported me into heaven to a place I call the weeping room. This happened back in 2003 when I was in Seattle, Washington. I was praying in a small room when I felt the power of God come. Suddenly I felt a similar sensation as in previous times when I was taken up in the spirit. It felt like I was being catapulted through time and space. Again, I looked to my left and saw a mighty angel taking me by my left hand.

It appeared to be the same angel who had transported me into the very presence of Jesus when I was in Newfoundland in 2001, so I wasn't fearful, only astonished. For two minutes or so this angel took me straight up through the realms of the spirit, through the heavenly realms. I saw the earth growing smaller and smaller below me. As this angel took me to the place where I landed, once again I fell upon my knees.

The instant I came to my senses, if you will, in this place I could feel the love of God. But this time I felt a sadness and compassion that I'd never experienced before. As I began to look around the room, I saw four mighty angels stationed at the cardinal points of this room. I began to hear someone praying loudly in the Holy Spirit. But I fell upon my face and began to weep because of the incredible glory and presence of God's ultimate compassion that I felt in this place. I sensed a supernatural compassion and almost a sense of heartbreak in the room.

This whole time as the glory and power of God hovered around me, I was aware that these four angelic beings were there on guard. They were mighty! They were all enrobed in white garments with swords and shields, and they all had the countenance of might and power. I knew that these were some of God's most powerful warrior angels, and I knew that they were stationed in this place to guard something very, very special.

I lay upon the floor. I could see that the floor was made of wood; it appeared to be knotty pine with a very thick resin on it. It was the color of gold but it was wood. As I lay there, I could feel the compassion of God wash through me in wave after wave after wave after wave. I stayed in that place for a long time and wept and wept and wept. My tears filled my eyes then dribbled down off my nose and off of my cheeks and formed a pool on the knotty pine floor. (I am not sure but my tears may have been upon the earth and not falling in the heavenly realms.) From time to time I would raise my head just a bit and look at the angels. They were stationed in military fashion, in precision and on guard.

Finally after about forty minutes, I sat up and pulled myself up to my knees. I saw a large four-poster bed in the room and heard the voice of someone praying in a language that I did not understand. And when I looked to the bed, I saw the Lord. Jesus was sitting upon this bed! It was quite large, about ten feet long and eight feet wide. The Lord had His back turned to me. I could see His white robe. I knew it was the Lord because as He prayed I could see the nail scar in His left hand. I felt the compassion of Christ. He was weeping and crying and praying for the lost. He was weeping and crying and praying for the widows and orphans of the earth (Romans 8:26-27).

At that moment Jesus turned and looked over His left shoulder and motioned for me to come to Him. As I approached Jesus, I knelt down at His feet and began to weep. The Lord put His hand upon me. The second that Jesus touched me, I went out into visions of God and I began to see thousands of children. It was as if a movie reel flashed through my mind. Every instant another person would come forward—a child, a widow, an orphan. And every time I saw a face, I knew exactly their circumstances. I knew if they were hungry; I knew if they were being tormented; I knew if they were being abused; I knew everything that they were feeling.

And I knew at that moment that Jesus was interceding for His friends upon earth (Romans 8:27; John 17:20-23). Something was birthed within my heart. I watched these faces unfold in front of me for what seemed like hours, thousands and thousands of faces. In the end the Lord looked at me and asked me to stand. He held me close to His breast. And the Lord was weeping and I was weeping because I felt the compassion that Jesus exudes for these precious people. The tears of the Lord Jesus flowed down His nose and trickled onto my face.

The Lord birthed in me a desire to help those who couldn't help themselves. The Lord held me in His arms for the longest time. Finally He told me to go. He said, "You know what to do."

I turned and left. As I walked away from the Lord, I found myself once again being transported back through time and space. And once again this mighty angel was there, taking me by my left hand. And once again I saw the earth come into view below. I saw the tiny room where I had been. And suddenly I was sucked back into my body. I lay there for hours weeping, as God had birthed within me compassion for the weak and helpless.

My friend, God wants us to be a father to the fatherless and the least of these (Matthew 10:42; 25:40). He wants us to go and find those people who He wants to touch and help minister to. When we give a cup of cold water to a child, we give it to Jesus. When we go out into the streets and feed the hungry, we feed Jesus. My friend, I believe God has angels like this that can take you into the realms of heaven, into the very presence Jesus where God can transform your mindset and supernaturally birth within you a hunger and a passion to see the lost saved and to see the poor and the destitute ministered to with the love of God the Father. This is pure and undefiled religion (James 1:27).

## CHAPTER 11

# Born to Encounter Him
# by Robert Ward

There are times when the Lord encounters us sovereignly and other times when we initiate the encounter. What I'm going to share with you is a time when I seized the moment and laid hold of what the Lord has promised to us as believers. There is a reality of the Kingdom of God that is in every believer that I will be conversing about in this chapter.

I was flying from a conference in North Carolina. And I was starting the second leg of my trip from Newark, New Jersey, to San Francisco, California. I went ahead and got comfortable to engage heaven and get lost in the reality of the goodness of our Father. I put some worship music on to set my mind on things above (Colossians 3:2). It is here when I forget this world and completely become submerged in my Father's. I started to engage heaven, started to engage the presence of the Lord.

I began to become enraptured by His presence, a world where there is no awareness of corruption and sin. A world that He has given us access through Jesus Christ; where we can boldly come before the throne because of the blood of our King, Jesus (Ephesians 3:12; Hebrews 4:14–16).

Jesus is the way, the truth, and the life; no one can come to the Father but through Him (John 14:6). Where is our Father? Our Father is in His dominion, His home, which is heaven. What has Jesus given us access too? I know this is a hard one because He has given us the potential to many things and we could not count them all.

Jesus repeatedly said the Kingdom of God is at hand, it has come near (Matthew 4:17; Mark 1:15; Luke 10:9). I want you to think about what Jesus has given us entry into with His death, resurrection, ascension, and glorification. He has appointed us a new home as a believer. This home is mentioned in the Epistles of Paul. One of them is in Ephesians where Paul writes we are seated with Him in the heavenly places in Christ Jesus (Ephesians 2:6). This means whether we like it or not we are functioning from a different place, from a contrasting world, a different realm (John 15:19; 17:16)—in our Father's world, in Jesus, where there is no corruption, no chaos.

It's important that we understand that when our Father's Kingdom comes and is released on the earth that something has to move. Both of those worlds cannot have dominion at the same time. In other words, when our Father's world is displayed, when heaven is released, or the Kingdom of God, either His domain will take over or the chaos will reign. We know that the Father's dominion takes over wherever it goes. When the Prince of Peace, Jesus, displays Himself and peace touches chaos, heaven touches earth; that peace will dominate. Peace is not an absence of conflict but the residue of the world that our King carries with Him wherever He goes.

It was here that I became immersed in the presence of the Lord, the Father's world. The Kingdom of God is in the presence of the Lord (Romans 14:17). Whenever we experience one aspect or part of His Kingdom, we are experiencing His nature and who He is. It is highly similar to a friend who is experiencing the daily activities of a person by tasting of their world—where they work, where they go throughout the day, their general activities. When someone does that with another person, they are encountering who that other person is by experiencing their world. It is very similar to us tasting and seeing the Lord is good in His Kingdom and us knowing the Lord through that (Psalm 34:8), because to know Him is eternal life (John 17:3). Any encounter and experience with the Lord or His Kingdom is for us to know who He is, His nature, how His world functions so that we can display heaven on earth.

As I listened to worship on the plane, I knew that I had several hours to feed on the faithfulness of God and remember all the great things that He had done for me and those around me during that conference (Psalm 37:3). I began to feel the presence of the Lord begin to envelope me (Psalm 91:1). This was the beginning of the encounter. I was looking to dive deep into the presence of the Lord, which includes His Kingdom.

Sometimes friends can initiate encounters or meetings with each other (John 15:15). The interesting thing about friends is they choose to be together. And occasionally a friend would say to another friend, "I want to meet you for a meal or tea." And that friend would invite another friend to be with him or her. As we draw near to Him, He draws near to us (James 4:8). Often the Lord is inviting us to initiate the encounter in a sense of choosing to draw near to Him so He will draw near to us. That is what I was doing. I wasn't waiting around for the Lord to randomly encounter me; I initiated it, like I have done so many other times by drawing near to Him in my heart and then waiting for Him to respond to my invitation.

And like He does routinely, He responded to my heart's desire to encounter Him and know Him further. My original intent to encounter Him was to give thanks to Him personally for the copious things He had done over the handful of days at the conference. As I felt the Lord overshadow and envelope me, I began to become more and more lost in the presence of the Lord; and it was as if my consciousness was submerged in Him and Him in me (John 14:20; 1 John 4:15). It seems like I was 95 percent in the Father's world, in the presence of the Lord. And I was conscious only 5 percent on this earth. I began to feel the love of God surround me like I was in a deep ocean and every water molecule was His love (1 John 4:16). I began to focus on the presence of the Lord that was surrounding me. As I did I became increasingly lost in His goodness and kindness (Romans 2:4). It is far greater than anything on the face of this earth. His love is pure and undefiled, and I felt there was no requirement from me to pay Him back in some way for what He was releasing to me. In other words there was no room for "I will do this for you, so you will now do this for Me." It was pure and alive (Hebrews 4:12).

When the Lord encounters you or you experience Him in some way, He is inviting you into a place where you realize that you abide in Him, abide in His love (John 15:10). He is ushering you into a place where you realize that He loves you and to come into the revelation that "*We love, because He first loved us*" (1 John 4:19, NASB); not through head knowledge but through an encounter of the person of Jesus, where the experience of the love of God, through encounter, changes and transforms us from glory to glory (2 Corinthians 3:18). And we are moved into who the Father says we are; not our personal beliefs, which are dictated occasionally through what others have said about us or events or circumstances in our lives. The Lord wants His world to be an actual reality to us so we can do what the Father is doing (John 5:19).

It is through experiencing Him that we better know who He is and His nature to display it on the earth, to display heaven on earth. But this happens through encountering Him. As I was getting lost in the presence of the Lord, His being began to completely surround me. And I began to *see*, though my eyes were closed and I had my headphones on engaged in worship with the Lord. I began to see a white tunnel in front of me; and I was catapulted into it, moving through it for several seconds with numerous turns and movements. As though I was on a rollercoaster, it moved exceedingly fast through the turns; and I was in awe as I was being moved through this white tunnel. Then I realized that it was coming to an end and I was shot out of it.

It was as if I was being shot out of a cannon, the movement was so fast and seemed very precise. I was thrown into an open area where there was a purple mist that was two or three feet high. And there was a feeling of homage and royalty as I moved into the purple mist that was on the floor, which seemed it had no end as it stretched from all corners till I could not see into the distance anymore. This feeling of majesty was so tangible. I was in a sense tasting of it, experiencing it. It was more than just a normal episode; the feeling penetrated every part of my being. In a way I became a part of the royalty that was surrounding me and it became a part of me.

As I looked at the indigo mist, I became enraptured in the goodness of our Father, feeling and tasting of the glory and majesty of our King. I heard once that a picture is worth a thousand words. This experience was so vivid and unmistakable that it had a substance and emotion not common to this world. As though my senses were overloaded, the intensity was so strong that I could not focus on one thing as it engulfed me—Jesus standing in the indigo mist, having weight and movement, foreign in the natural. He stood gazing at me with an intense love that overpowered me to bow in His presence. The authority that enclosed Him was mighty, and it seemed everything and anything moved at the sound of His word or thought. This atmosphere encompassing Him understood His kingship and supremacy. It was waiting for the very command of its Maker, with an uncanny knowing Jesus was the Author and Creator. He was in charge but did not have to show or display it outwardly. Everything around Him recognized it, including me. There were feelings of peace, tangible yet light in weight. The King of Glory was present and the whole of creation seemed to be bowing to Him in every possible way. His love was strong it crippled me to the floor, and the honor He carried was heavy in weight but it was invisible and yet evident.

As I was being overwhelmed by the love and glory of the environment that I was in, I looked up gazing in astonishment at the King of Glory, Jesus Christ, standing just a short distance from me, maybe ten or fifteen feet away. He was standing in the mist wearing a white robe that went down to His feet. And at that moment I could do nothing but fall on my face because of the glory and love that surrounded Him; it was so overwhelming, so robust. I was at a loss for words, absent for action. I was in complete awe now of His kingship, His authority, His duty, His royalty. And coupled with all of this, His love permeated every part of those characteristics. I could do nothing but worship the Lord in His glory, in His love for me. I was without words as I set my desire to express my adoration to Him merely through thought and intent. As I was there for a few moments, I was lost in the majesty of our King.

Jesus said nothing, He had no need to; who He was resonated from His being. The King of kings the Lord of lords was present. No one needed to explain it; there was a knowing in that realm—a knowing that Jesus was "I AM" (John 8:58; John 18:5). He seemed to vibrate the concept "I AM the Alpha and Omega" without saying any words (Revelation 1:8; 21:6; 22:13). The indigo mist was gorgeous; it was like a garment that surrounded Him, somehow connected to Him though He was not wearing it. I had a sense that it moved and followed Him wherever He went in this place. The glory He carried was magnificent and was interlaced with His kingship. There are not enough words to describe what was happening in that world; His presence was beautiful, heavy, and glorious. He is the King and it seemed to flow from His surroundings—more in a sound, movement, and weight; not in language.

I discovered something there I never knew before. It was the kingship our Lord Jesus carries. I could not have learned this in a book. It seems it would have taken years for me to learn the knowledge that I received from that experience. It happened in merely a few seconds in the natural but felt like an eternity in that realm. Our Lord carries an authority He gave to us also, that we may display His world here on earth. I tasted of it knowing this is the same authority He gave to His believers, His children, so we may transform this world from His world; this is what the Lord has assigned to us. Through encounter, the release of His presence within every believer, we will change the world together with Him. It is not that He needs our help, but it is the fact He chose to partner with humanity to transform the world, bringing the realities of heaven here on this planet.

I had a knowing that I was in the presence of the Lord before I saw Him. His love, reputation, and splendor preceded Him. It was enough to be in His company. There was a satisfaction that was not of this world. In the presence of our Almighty King, I bowed and worshiped Him; not out of obligation but because I couldn't help myself, His love was so potent and mighty. It was fierce and seemed to say, "When you come near Me you will taste of My affection for you." Lost in the beauty of our King, the presence that surrounded Him was so sublime that I just basked and bathed in it. As I waited, I was suddenly taken out, and I became more conscious of the reality on earth than the Kingdom of God within me.

There was something that I tasted, that I could not learn just by knowledge. But through the encounter, I stepped into a greater knowing of who He is and His realm. Whatever Jesus did He empowered His disciples to do likewise. He said He was the light of the world while He told His disciples, "*You are the light of the world*" (John 8:12; Matthew 5:14). He healed sickness and disease and casted out demons. Then He gave His disciples power and authority over every kind of sickness and disease and over all demons (Matthew 10:1; Luke 9:1). Whenever the Lord demonstrates something to me, such as His love, His healing nature, His grace, His mercy, whatever it may be; He always tells me, "Go and do likewise. Now go and display this to others and show them what I have shown you by giving that to them (Luke 6:31). Love as I have loved you. Give as I have given to you" (Matthew 10:8).

The Lord is ushering His people into encounter, a posture and position where we can taste and see the Lord is good. He is saying to us that sometimes He will initiate the encounter but He wants us to know that we have the ability and permission to draw near to Him; to come boldly before the throne because of the access we have through Jesus Christ. He is saying, "Come and see what friendship looks like with Me." And in that friendship we have influence and permission to His heart. Not because He had to, but because He chose to allow us to have influence. Today I want you to know that you were born for encounter; you were born to experience the Kingdom of God, that is His world which is within you (Luke 17:21).

Sometimes when I have an encounter with the Lord I do not learn as I do in the natural through knowledge first; it is more knowledge gained through an experience. I believe He showed me the authority and majesty that every believer carries because of how Jesus empowered us. I feel strongly, one of the best ways for us to come into the fullness of all He gave to us is realized by us understanding His nature through experiencing Him. The Lord has set us up for encounter as a disciple of Jesus. You were created to know Him as a friend knows another friend (Exodus 33:11).

## Activation Prayer:

*Father, I pray You would open the realms of Your world to us; that we would know You more intimately so we may display Your heart and Your Kingdom on this earth. Lord, may we see from Your perspective the authority and majesty each believer carries as a child of God. Father, may You show us what it is like to be a friend of God and how a friend interacts with You. I thank You, Lord, You no longer call us servants but friends. I thank You, Father, we are not of this world as You are not of this world. Show us, Jesus, what it means to be in You and to have You in us. Father, I surrender to all You have for my life and the full inheritance that we have in Christ Jesus.*

## CHAPTER 12

# Singing With Angels in Malawi

In 2003 I was in Malawi, Africa, helping lead ministry teams and outreaches in the city. During this time the Lord began to lead me to pray again. In fact, for the first four days I was in Malawi, I did not sleep. The Holy Spirit would lead me to pray. I would pray up into the night as He led, often times praying in the Holy Ghost. During these times the Holy Spirit spoke to me.

The first night we were at the Sunbird Capital Hotel, the Holy Spirit said, "Kevin, I want you to go out into the garden and worship me in spirit and in truth" (John 4:24). So I went out into the garden and began to sing in the spirit and to worship God. Over the course of the next three nights, the Lord had me go to the garden each night. During this time as I prayed in the Spirit and danced and worshiped in the spirit, I began to sense angels dancing in unison with me. I could also hear the angels singing in unison with me. Soon I realized that I was able to hear the voices of the angels as I worshiped God in spirit and in truth, as I danced in a circle in the garden at the Sunbird Capital Hotel, dancing with all of my might like a little child before God.

Dancing and skipping in a circle and singing in the Holy Spirit, I began to realize that angels were singing with me. Over the course of three nights, God began to open up my ears and eyes; I began to hear the angels and then I began to see the angels. At first the angelic singing was faint, but it grew louder over time. After three evenings in the garden in the cool of the day I could begin to hear God's angels singing around me very clearly. There were dozens of angels. I would dance in a counterclockwise direction singing in the spirit and the angels would dance in a clockwise direction singing in the spirit. After a while I could hear them clearly, I could see them clearly.

It became exciting to go to the garden at night to sing and worship God in spirit and truth because I was singing with angels and the angels were singing with me. As I would dance I would look at the angels and I began to recognize the angels. These were worship angels. They had instruments and they were singing in their heavenly language. As we danced and praised God, the glory and power of God began to build. The fragrance of frankincense, myrrh, and calamas would invade the area.

On the fourth night I fell to my knees weeping. I fell down upon my knees crying out to God, worshiping Him and thanking Him for everything that He was doing, for all the miracles that were happening. Suddenly I felt the power and unconditional love of Jesus. And I looked up to see my Savior. There He was; the Jesus was standing in right front of me. At first this was an open vision. Jesus reached out with His right hand, and the angels were still dancing and were still singing.

When Christ appeared in the circle and touched me with His right hand, I had revelation that I was to be His hands and feet on the continent of Africa in many nations at many different times. The Lord spoke to me and gave me direction. I closed my eyes and began to weep. I opened my eyes and the Lord was gone but His angels were still dancing, His angels were still singing.

My friend, we can dance and sing with God's angels. We can worship God in spirit and truth. And your life can be transformed as you learn to worship the Father, as you learn to worship the Son, as you learn to worship the Holy Spirit in spirit and in truth. The Lord can open up the eyes of your heart to see God's angels who are always worshiping Him. And in those times you, too, can have visitations of Jesus that can change your life. My friends, dancing with angels is something anyone can do, and I believe God wants you to dance with His angels too. You can learn to entertain heaven too.

## CHAPTER 13

# Kathy's Guardian Angel

Guardian angels are the most accepted form of angelic ministry in the world. I believe that everyone has at least one guardian angel. Nearly every denomination has faith for and believes in guardian angels. This is a well-accepted doctrine in the Body of Christ today, and even in the world.

Jesus talked about guardian angels in Matthew 18. He called a little child to Himself, and then He set the child in the midst of the disciples. He said, "*Assuredly, I say to you* [I tell you the truth], *unless you are converted and become as little children, you will by no means* [not] *enter in to the kingdom of heaven. Therefore whoever humbles himself as this little child is the greatest in the kingdom of heaven. Whoever receives one little child like this in My name receives Me*" (Matthew 18:3).

Later on He taught about guardian angels when He said this: "*Take heed that you do not despise one of these little ones* [children], *for I say to you* [tell you the truth] *that in heaven their angels always see the face of My Father who is in heaven*" (v. 10). Jesus teaches us that little children have angels that are assigned to them. These angels (perhaps guardian angels) are released to stand before the Father on behalf of the child.

So my question for you is this; just because you grow up to be adults, does that mean you lose your angel which God has assigned to you as a child? An angel who always beholds the face of our Father who is in heaven? The answer is no. We all have at least one guardian angel, in my opinion. I also believe that it is possible that some people have numerous angels assigned to them on this side of eternity.

## A Big Kiss from Heaven

In 2007 Kathy and I were in Tanzania conducting crusades (Gospel outreach meetings) in seven cities in the Lakes District near Lake Victoria. We saw God do a lot of amazing miracles and were given the grace to lead an estimated 19,000 precious people to receive Jesus as Lord and Savior in those seven weeks. I give God all the glory for those things! During that time there was a lot of warfare, so Kathy gave herself to intercession on a daily basis. I thank God for that!

One day I had been in a meeting with pastors in the city and I came back to hotel. It was a hot day, about 100 degrees. There on the stoop of the steps that led to our little room I saw Kathy. She looked so beautiful! She was wearing a white outfit, and in the hot African sun she seemed to glow. I thought to myself, "She looks so beautiful! When I get over there I'm going to give her a big hug and a big kiss and I'm going to tell her how much I love her." But I also thought it was a bit unusual that she was outside in the hot African sun because Kathy likes to protect herself from the sunshine and it is quite intense in Africa.

I waved at her and smiled and she waved back to me and smiled back and gave me the biggest beautiful smile that I'd seen her give me in a long time. Our eyes locked for a few seconds and I thought; "Kathy sure looks extra beautiful today!" It seemed that she was very excited to see me! I couldn't wait to get to her so I could hug her and kiss her and just tell her how much I love her and appreciate her. I walked around a plant to get to the other side of the stoop. But when I got there, there was no Kathy! She was gone! One instant she was there and the next instant she was gone! It seemed that she had vanished in plain sight! There seemed to be a lingering sense of holiness in the air around the steps.

I quickly bounded up the stairs and tried to open the door to our little room, but it was locked. So I fumbled with the key, I unlatched the door, I walked in, and I said, "Honey, how did you get in here so fast?" She was lying on the bed and I knew she was praying. When I looked at her, I realized she was wearing khaki pants; she didn't have on a white outfit. At that moment it dawned on me that I had seen Kathy's guardian angel. She said, "What are you talking about?" I said, "Honey, I just saw your guardian angel." Then I told her the testimony.

My friends, I want you to know something. God's angels perform His word. I knew Kathy had been praying for our protection. As we decree God's word over our life, we empower God's angels to move and work on our behalf. God's angels often work to protect us and guard us from harm or danger. As we decree God's word over our life, we empower God's angels to minister for us. At times God's angels minister for us by guarding us and protecting us.

This is the dynamic that we see outlined in Psalm 91:11-12: *"For He shall give His angels charge over you, To keep you in all your ways. In their hands they shall bear you up, Lest you dash your foot against a stone."* God will give His angels charge over us. God has angels He wants to empower in your life through your words and through your prayers too!

CHAPTER 14

# Warrior Angels in Tanzania

On Tuesday, the 28th of May in 2002, I was in Mwanza, Tanzania. God had supernaturally opened up doors for me of provision and favor, allowing me the resources and the wherewithal to take a missions trip to Africa. These marvelous blessings were the direct result of angelic ministry and intervention in my life.

In this place the spirit of prayer came upon me and I began to understand what the Book of Romans is talking about when it says the Spirit makes utterances through us which we cannot understand (8:26). The spirit of prayer came upon me about midnight, and I began to pray and intercede, praying in the Holy Spirit. My mentor, Omega Dowell, had sent anointing oil with me saying, "Brother Kevin, you will find a good use for this in Africa!" I prayed for hours and hours, anointing the room with oil and praying. God began to bring faces to my mind, and I would pray and intercede for those individuals. Finally, after about four and a half hours, I put a chair in the middle of the room and I knelt upon the cold tile floor of bungalow number

6 at the Tilapia Hotel. I put my elbows upon the seat of the chair and continued to pray.

Suddenly I began to feel the manifest glory of God as it began to filter into the room. First it was like little wavelets would hit my knees. As time passed the little wavelets of glory became higher and higher, until after twenty or thirty minutes the glory of God had increased greatly. A wave came in and hit me up above my waist and literally knocked me from my kneeling position with my elbows on the chair to the floor. But when I hit the floor, I didn't fall upon a musty tile floor in a bungalow in the nation of Tanzania. I fell upon a perfumed beach by a sea of glass like crystal in the heavenly realms.

I couldn't move. The water gently billowed around me as the warm crystal clear water of the sea washed around my body. I lay there for a long time unable to move. I could smell the fragrance of frankincense and myrrh and I could hear angelic worship. It was very similar to the angelic worship I had heard at Living Waters Church in Springdale in Newfoundland, Canada.

I began to examine my surroundings as these waves of God's glory would wash around me on this beach. The beach was made of rubies and diamonds and pearls. Eventually, as I was washed around by God's glory, I could see the crystal clear waters of the sea of glass like crystal. I began to watch them as the luminescence of the light that illuminated this wonderful place seemed to dance and to move with the angelic worship that seemed to fill the air of this wonderful place. I lay there and I thought about how wonderful Jesus is.

I was no longer in my body; I was no longer in Tanzania. I was in heavenly places. Soon I began to see the sun arise over the sea of glass like crystal. Let me say that this was not a sun like we see at the center of our solar system. No, this was a supernatural Son. And as this sun arose, incredible colors began to dance between the sky and the sea. The sea reflected the colors of the sky and the sky reflected the phosphorescent colors of the sea. I watched this unfold for what seemed like hours, breathing in the fragrance of frankincense and myrrh and luxuriating in the wavelets of glory that washed over my body.

Suddenly I saw a shadow appear; it blocked out the light of the sun. I was disappointed. As I watched the shadow, I realized it was moving closer to me until finally I realized it was the silhouette of a man. Then my mind had instantaneous revelation; it was Jesus! He overshadowed me as He was walking across the sea of glass like crystal. He continued walking in my direction. I watched as the Lamb of God walked the last few feet across the crystal clear water, stepped upon the beach, and walked up and stood over me. The Lord overshadowed me at that moment (Matthew 17:8).

I gazed into the eyes of God—the precious, beautiful eyes of Jesus, pools of living love. The Lord looked at me and smiled. Once again I felt His unconditional love as it washed over me, as it enveloped me. His amazing love healed and cleansed me. I thought, "It's so wonderful to be back in the presence of Jesus."

And then Jesus began to speak to me. He began to tell me about the seers. He began to tell me about the seer prophets of old. After a while the Lord stopped speaking to me. I was quite disappointed because I was fixed on and glued to every word He was teaching me about His Kingdom.

## Releasing Angels Into the Nations

Suddenly the Lord looked up and He looked off to His right. I was disappointed but I was also curious. At that moment I saw a large angel jog up to Jesus and stop. The Lord looked at this angel with interest and they began to speak in a language that I didn't understand. After a moment or two Jesus took His right hand and He patted this angel on his left shoulder. He had to reach up to do it because this angel was probably nine or ten feet tall. I could tell that he had been involved in warfare. His shield was dented, his robe was a bit dirty, and I could tell he was a little weary. But he was also elated to see Jesus. The Lord spoke one last thing to him. I watched in amazement as this angel ascended up into the heavens on Jesus.

Then the Lord looked at me. In my mind I thought, "I hope He continues to speak to me." He smiled and He told me not to fear. He continued to tell me things. In a few moments I was astonished again as I saw an angel descend upon Jesus. This angel looked fresh and crisp and clean and energetic. It had on a white robe with a golden belt. On the belt was a small assortment of weaponry. He had a large two-edged sword with a big handle on it. He had a shield and his arms were clad in armor. He was excited to be there with the Lord.

Once again Jesus began to speak to this angel in a language I didn't understand. The angel shook his head up and down as if he were receiving instructions and indicated that he was understanding them. It occurred to me that Jesus Christ is the Lord of Hosts and at that moment the Lord of Hosts was releasing His angelic hosts into the kingdoms of earth. After a moment the Lord patted this angel on his shoulder. This mighty warrior angel then spun around in military precision and rushed off, as if on an assignment.

And I had the revelation that Jesus Christ was at that moment releasing angels into the nations of Africa. These angels were being sent forth to minister over nations, over cities, over ministers, over churches to help bring forth God's purposes and plans in those places. I watched as Jesus interacted with hundreds of angels—angels of different size, different stature. These angels had different levels of authority and different levels of command in Christ's army. I watched as Jesus commanded each of these angels to go out into the realms of earth throughout Africa; each garbed with weapons of warfare; each instructed by Jesus the Lord of Hosts giving them detailed instructions about what they were to do, where they were to do it, how they were to do it, and who they were to minister for.

During this same time I saw hundreds of angels return from various efforts and various areas of Africa. They, too, were debriefed by Jesus. Each one appeared to be a bit weary from the battle, but each one was also elated to see Jesus. In turn I saw each angel ascend into the heavens on Christ.

My friend, God has millions of angels like this that He wants to send forth to minister for those who are heirs of salvation. You can call upon the name of the Lord and He can release legions of angels to minister for you. Remember what Jesus said in the Book of Matthew 26:53: *"Do you think that I cannot now pray to My Father, and He will provide Me with more than twelve legions of angels?"*

Saints, I believe I saw some of the legions of God's angels ascending upon Jesus returning to heaven and descending upon the Lord and going out unto the earth to minister on missions of mercy. Twelve legions of angels equal 72,000 angels. I believe that God has given us the authority to work or co-labor with His angels, to loose or activate them out into the realms of earth as the Father and the Holy Spirit will.

I don't understand exactly what happened, but I know that I saw Jesus release His angels to do His bidding upon the earth. I pondered this experience in my heart for over a year, asking God for confirmation. The Holy Spirit led me to the Book of John 1:51. Jesus said the day will come when you will see *"the angels of God ascending and descending upon the Son of Man."*

Saints, I believe that's what I experienced. And I believe you can have similar experiences too. Perhaps you can one day see the angels of God ascending and descending upon the Son of Man yourself.

## CHAPTER 15

# Guardian Angels in Murchison Falls, Uganda

In 2002 I found myself in Africa for the second time. This was the fulfillment of a prophetic promise that Jesus gave me on Killick Island near Bay Roberts, Newfoundland, Canada. It was upon Killick Island where I had a visitation of the Holy Spirit and the Lord commissioned me to travel to Africa to preach His Gospel and minister in healing. I'll skip the multitude of miracles that happened as God allowed me to activate or loose the angel of provision that He had released to me in the realms of heaven I wrote of earlier in this book. I was able to release the same angel to prosper my business as God allowed me to garner the necessary finances to pay for these missions trips to Africa. It all transpired in a most supernatural fashion, and I am still praising God for these miracles today! The funds for the entire missions trip came into my hands in less than twenty-four hours.

On this particular trip I was helping lead a mission team of about forty people. We had gone on a two-day safari into Murchison Falls National Park. We were staying at the game lodge at Murchison Falls. Again, the spirit of prayer and intercession came upon me and I began to intercede at about eleven o'clock at night. At the park they cut the generator off that supplies the electricity, so I lit a candle. I was praying in the middle of a round hut that was about twenty-five feet in circumference. I was in the room alone. I began to intercede as the Holy Spirit led me. It was a glorious time of seeking the Lord's face.

Suddenly the spirit of prayer intensified upon me and I began to pray in the Holy Spirit. As I would pray, once again I would see the faces of people; some that I knew and some that I didn't know. I would pray in the Holy Spirit and I would pray in English with understanding. It seemed that the Lord had me praying for protection over individuals on our team, and for the missions trip in general.

The next day it turned out that we all needed protection as we became stranded in the game preserve in the midst of a torrential downpour. Both of our vehicles became stuck in mud on the slick orange Ugandan dirt roads. Through the grace of God and angelic ministry, we were able to leave the park at 4 a.m.; but not until I had seen God release about forty mighty angels to stand behind the missions team and help them to push the bus out of a mud pit. In the natural this would have been totally impossible for humans to free such a large bus from such a ditch with their own strength.

As I continued to pray and intercede, time passed quickly. I prayed in the Holy Spirit for about four and a half hours. Somewhere around 4:30 or 5:00 a.m., I began to feel the anointing and power of God manifest in the little hut. I began to smell the fragrance of frankincense and myrrh. I could actually feel wind blowing inside the little hut in a circular motion. So for a moment I opened my eyes and looked; the little candle that I had lit on the table across from the bed was actually flickering in the breeze. I closed my eyes and continued to pray just in the Holy Spirit; really just worshiping God, thanking Him for another opportunity to travel to Africa and to preach His word to His precious people there.

Once again I felt an increase in the power of God. I felt as if the wind blowing in the room increased. I opened my eyes again to look at the candle. When I did I saw four strong angels standing in the mud hut. It appeared that they were stationed at cardinal points. I looked at these angels with astonishment. I was glad they were there because I knew these angels were mighty warrior angels; these were guardian angels. I didn't know exactly what they were there to guard, but I knew that somehow as I had prayed in the Holy Spirit I had loosed or activated these angels of God from the heavenly realms.

I believe as we pray according to Jude 1:20, as we pray in the Holy Spirit, at times we are activating and loosing God's angels to do things for God's people and to manifest things on earth as it is in heaven. I examined these angels; they all appeared to be about nine feet tall. They had different colored hair; most were blonde, some had brown hair. One particularly strong angel seemed to have bright red hair like that of an Irishmen. They were all mighty; they actually looked a little like Vikings. They had shields and swords and were at attention. It was clear to me that they were on high alert and ready for action. All of these angels that came to our aid were well built and very muscular and they looked like weight lifters!

This gave me a great sense of peace. I closed my eyes again, smiling and thanking God for His angels as I continued to pray. After a few moments the intense fragrance of the Lord multiplied in the room. Then there was actually a knock on my door. I stopped praying in the Spirit because I was praying out loud. I thought someone had come to the door of the hut. Then I heard a voice say, "Kevin!" So I listened, expecting someone to knock on the door again. But no one knocked. In a moment I heard the voice say, "Kevin!" I realized that it was the Lord and He was speaking to me. So, I responded in an audible voice, "Yes, Lord!" He said this three times.

Then Jesus spoke to me in a clear voice; as a matter of fact, it is most likely that He spoke to me in an audible voice. He said, "Kevin, when the time is right, you must move to Kansas City, Missouri. You are to submit to the authority of Christ Triumphant Church. You are to submit to the authority of the pastors there. It's important that you do this." "Do you understand?" He asked. I answered, "Yes, Lord." Then the Lord said, "Your ministry must go through Kansas City." I said, "Yes, Lord."

And then it seemed as if the presence of the Lord lifted. I opened my eyes and looked. I could see the four angels; they were still standing at attention, action ready. I continued to pray and give God glory.

It was later that morning that we prepared for another short safari. Then later that afternoon, as we left, it began to rain heavily. On the trip out as our vehicles became stuck and mired in the mud, God opened up my spiritual eyes. I saw as the men from the missions team stood around the bus up to their ankles in mud trying to push the bus out of the muddy quagmire, angels suddenly appeared behind them. It was like the bus popped out of the mud like a butterfly would push out of its cocoon.

A man named Dave Duke from Canada began to drive the bus supernaturally over the soggy, muddy roads in the bush of Uganda. At times the bus would slide; at one point it actually slid 180 degrees and we were sliding sideways down the center of the muddy road. I was standing behind Dave looking and praying as he was driving. For a moment the Lord opened my spiritual eyes. As I looked out the window, I saw those same mighty angels. They simply nudged the bus and it supernaturally flipped back into the right direction and we continued to drive perfectly down the center of the road until we found the paved tarmac and made it out of the bush at about 5 a.m.

Saints, let me tell you something. It is important that we pray in the Holy Spirit; it's important that we build ourselves up as we pray in the Holy Spirit. At times, as we do, we are activating and loosing God's angels to minister on our behalf and on the behalf of others. Praying in the Holy Spirit is key to activating angelic ministry in your life. I believe the Lord sent those four sentinel angels in advance of His coming to speak to me in that little mud hut.

So, once again, when God begins to speak to you and asks you to do what seems to be absurd things, be obedient. As you are obedient to go to one place, God will open up the double door for your destiny in Him. I encourage you to listen and to be obedient in these things. God often reveals His Kingdom and His plans for you line upon line and precept upon precept. As you are obedient to the first thing, the Lord will reveal the next step of His plan for you and your destiny in Him. This kind of revelation can come line upon line and precept upon precept (Isaiah 28:10).

## CHAPTER 16

# Angel of the Burning Bush

Although I didn't actually see this angel myself, I want to share this testimony because it is a beautiful picture of redemption. The other reason that this is an important testimony is because, I believe, just as in the life of Jesus, at times we can enter into the open heavens and have our eyes activated to see God's angels by proximity. Just as the disciples saw angels when they were near Jesus at times, when God opens the heavens over a person's life and uses them in the gift of discerning of spirits and allows them to see His angels, sometimes the people who are near that person can also begin to see angels.

In 2003 the Lord had spoken to me to move and to live with my mother. My mother was getting to be a bit older and she was struggling with her faith. During the season that I was living in my mother's home, I began to fast and pray and seek the Lord. It soon became clear to me that God had moved me to my mother's house because He wanted me to share some truths from His word with her.

My mother was struggling with unforgiveness. I would speak to her about what God's word said; that it is absolutely critical that we learn to forgive those people who have wronged us. My mom and I talked about this many times for hours. She finally told me, "Kevin, I don't think I can forgive the people who have done terrible things to me or to my family." We ended our conversation one day as I told her, "Mom, please just pray about this. It's very important."

A couple of days later I woke up early in the morning and I heard sobbing. I went into the dining room and saw my mother sitting at the kitchen table. She had her Bible open and she was looking at the scriptures. I could tell that she had had a supernatural encounter because she was searching the scriptures to find confirmation of her spiritual experience, just as we had done as we studied God's word together. I looked at her and simply said, "Mom, is there anything you would like to tell me?" She said, "No, I just want to be alone." So I respected her space and allowed her to work this issue out on her own.

A few days later I woke up and again found Mom at the table with her Bible. She said, "Kevin, I think I might be losing my mind." I asked, "Mom, what are you talking about?" She responded, "I was thinking about what you told me about forgiveness. I've been reading the scriptures; and I saw where Jesus said if we don't forgive those who've wronged us, our heavenly Father won't forgive us. So, I called out to God. I said, 'God, You've got to help me with this!'"

She went on to tell me: "I was watching television and I had an unusual desire to get up and go stand at the kitchen window. Kevin, when I went to the kitchen window I felt the presence of God. I haven't felt God's presence like that since I was a little girl. When I looked out the window, I saw the azalea bush and it was burning!" She continued, "Kevin, there was a beautiful blue flame that seemed to engulf the azalea bush. I watched it for about an hour, and I felt the presence of God. I've never felt anything like that! After about half an hour, God started speaking to me." I said, "Mom, that's great! What did He say?"

She responded, "The Lord spoke to me out of the blue flame that was surrounding that bush, Kevin! And God told me that what His word said about forgiveness is true, that I needed to forgive those that had wronged me or my children. And so I began to pray, and I felt God's Spirit like I've never felt it. I forgave everyone that came into my mind. And a peace came into my heart, Kevin; and I believe God's done something wonderful! I believe that something has changed in my life. What do you think?" I said "Praise God, Mom! That is awesome! Let's get the Bible out and see what it says."

I turned instinctively to Exodus 3, telling Mom to look at what it said and read her verses 2 through 4:

> *And the Angel of the LORD appeared to him in a flame of fire from the midst of a bush. So he looked, and behold, the bush was burning with fire, but the bush was not consumed. Then Moses said, "I will now turn aside and see this great sight, why the bush does not burn." So when the LORD saw that he turned aside to look, God called to him from the midst of the bush and said, "Moses, Moses!" And he said, "Here I am."*

She sat across from me and said, "That is exactly what happened to me! I have been looking for something in the Bible to help me understand and confirm this; but I have been looking in the New Testament. I never thought to look in the Old Testament." Mom's countenance seemed to take on a new luster. She asked, "Do you really think that God would speak to me like that from a burning bush?" I laughed and said; "Sure, Mom, He loves you very much." Mom was about eighty-three when this happened; and from that day forward I saw a new tenderness and gentleness in her. I believe that the Lord spoke to my Mom just like He did Moses and prepared her heart to enter into her heavenly home. After that day from time to time I would find Mom at the kitchen window looking out at the azalea bush praying to the Lord. She was a new creation after that encounter.

After that day there was a tenderness and a peace that was in my mom's spirit that hadn't been there previously. Later my mom did pass away, but I had an opportunity to spend time with her in a hospital room. She was very sick in intensive care. One night about 2 a.m. she sat up in the bed and looked at the door. She said, "Kevin, look! Who are those two men dressed in white?"

I knew that she was seeing angels who had been sent on assignment to take her to heaven. The Book of Psalms says the death of God's saints is precious in His eyes (116:15). At times God sends His angels to escort His saints into the realms of heaven. The next night my mom sat up in the bed again. She said, "Look, honey, Jesus is here!" And I said, "Praise God, Mom!" She lay back down and went back to sleep. When my mother went on to be with the Lord a few days later, I had a peace and I rejoiced because I knew that God had done a work in her heart. And I knew that God had sent His angels to take her into the very presence of Jesus.

Saints, the Bible says that to be absent from the body is to be present with the Lord (2 Corinthians 5:8). I thank God that my mother is present with the Lord now. Perhaps you don't know Jesus as your Savior; but you can. Find a Bible and read the Book of Romans chapter 10. It says that if we believe in our heart that Jesus is the Son of God and we confess that with our mouth—if we say it out loud, we will be saved (v. 9). My prayer is that you will be saved. My prayer is that we will spend eternity together in paradise with Jesus. In fact, you can read the prayer of salvation in the end of this book and be saved right now!

## CHAPTER 17

# Mighty Harvester Angel—
# Bukoba, Tanzania

I have seen this angel several times in Africa, a few other times in South America, and once in India. Revelation 14:6-7 says:

> *I saw another angel flying in the midst of heaven, having the everlasting gospel to preach to those who dwell on the earth—to every nation, tribe, tongue, and people— saying with a loud voice, "Fear God and give glory to Him, for the hour of His judgment has come; and worship Him who made heaven and earth, the sea and springs of water."*

In 2006 we were conducting a missions trip to the nation of Tanzania. We went to the northwest area to a city named Bukoba. We loved the people in Bukoba. They love Jesus and they are hungry for the Gospel. We prepared a five-day miracle outreach in the city.

As we preached the Gospel, that very first night I sensed that a huge angel stepped onto the crusade grounds. The Lord opened my spiritual eyes and for about three to five seconds I saw a large angel standing at the rear of the crusade grounds. This angel appeared to be over one hundred and twenty-five feet tall. He was powerful, he was mighty, and he had in his right hand a huge two-edged sword. This sword must have been at least sixty to seventy feet in length. The angel was holding it out over the crusade grounds. This angel had long blonde hair, and he seemed to have a type of armor made of leather and what appeared to be gold. His belt was clad with various articles of war. In his left hand he held a huge, shiny golden sword.

I was mesmerized when I saw this angel, but I had great comfort knowing that the Lord had sent this angel. And I realized this was the type of angel that Revelation 14 speaks about—an angel who has the anointing or the duty to bring the everlasting Gospel to those of every nation.

Two nights later as I stood upon the platform, one of the team members, Robin, from London, England, came up and tugged my sleeve. She said, "Kevin! Kevin! There's a large angel out there." I said, "Praise God, Robin! Tell me about it later." Later she did share the testimony. God had opened up her spiritual eyes, and she saw this same angel. She was very excited about this and I was very grateful that God had opened her eyes to "see" in a new way.

Robin saw how this angel was ministering to the people. As I prayed for people for healing, the angel spread its wings out and wafted wind over the congregation at the outreach. Women came forward as he did this and they were miraculously and instantaneously healed of tumors. The tumors just dissolved!

This was similar to the time that I saw an angel like this in Singapore. But this one in Bukoba was the largest angel that I had ever seen. After these crusade meetings I began to study the word to see if there was any scriptural precedence for angels like this. I saw in 1 Chronicles 21 in the Old Testament when King David sinned by numbering the people, God had sent an angel that began to slay the people. If you read the description in the word of God, you will see that this angel was massive.

My friends, God has massive angels who inhabit heaven; and the hour is at hand when these angels will begin to invade our time and our space to help us to manifest Christ's Kingdom on earth.

CHAPTER 18

# The Guardian Angel— London, England

This next testimony is a beautiful little kiss from God and a testimony about His guardian angels and how they are close to us at all times.

In 2006 Kathy and I had been invited to minister in London, England. One afternoon we had a little extra time, so we were going to lunch with some of our friends from the Elim church at Clapham Common. As we were walking down the street, I could continually feel as though someone had put their hands upon my shoulders and I could feel the shadow of an angel's wings come over me.

Many times I stopped and turned around and looked to see who was touching me and who was behind me. But in each instance I saw no one. So I asked the Holy Spirit, "Lord, what is this? What am I experiencing?" The Lord responded, "Kevin, your guardian angel is walking behind you and he is protecting you."

Psalm 91:11-12 says, "[God] *shall give His angels charge over you, To keep you in all your ways. In their hands they shall bear you up, Lest you dash your foot against a stone.*" I didn't see any danger when I was in London during this time, but something very interesting happened. As we walked down the street, I felt the shadow of this angel's wings over me. I felt as if this angel had his wings sort of hovering over me as a hen does with her chicks to protect them.

A few moments later a man walked by. As he walked by I noticed the expression on his face. (People don't really make eye contact very much in London.) This man stopped, and then he looked at me. His mouth dropped open, and it seemed that his skin turned a little pale, and his eyes became very big and elated. It was actually a little comical! He just stared at me as he walked by. So I turned my head and I watched him walk by. Then he stopped and I stopped. He walked up to me and said, "Excuse me, sir. I don't know if you know this, but there is an awfully big angel walking behind you and he's got his wings spread out over your shoulders. I thought you might like to know that." I said, "Well, thank you, sir. I appreciate that."

Saints, God's angels are real and they are with us at all times. As I said, I believe everyone has at least one guardian angel. I believe in this instance God allowed me to know that His guardian angel was standing over me and guarding me lest I should dash my foot against a stone.

## CHAPTER 19

# The Mighty Angel of Australia

I believe this mighty angel I saw was the angel over Australia. This was an angel similar to the one in the previous testimony about the harvester angel.

In 1 Chronicles 21:16 after David had numbered the people, the Bible says, *"Then David lifted his eyes and saw the angel of the LORD standing between earth and heaven, having in his hand a drawn sword stretched out over Jerusalem. So David and the elders, clothed in sackcloth, fell on their faces."* David saw a big angel. And the Bible tells us that angel had slain tens of thousands of people (v. 14). But as they repented, God relented and the angel staid his hand (v. 15).

My friends, there are angels like this in the Kingdom of Heaven. There are angels that populate the heavenly realm that are massive and enormous in size. The way that I began to understand this aspect of the heavenly realms happened when I was in Australia in the city of Melbourne in late 2003. I was in a powerful service there where the glory of God and the anointing of the Holy Spirit were moving in power.

The Lord opened my spiritual eyes as I looked out the windows of this church on that Sunday morning, and I saw one leg of a massive angel. This angel appeared to be about one hundred feet tall or more. The Lord continued to open my spiritual eyes, and it was as if the structure of the building melted away and I was able to look up. It was as if I was looking up at this angel from my position at his foot and he stretched above my head and reaching into the clouds of the Australian sky! He was at least a hundred and twenty feet tall. He was powerful and he had long curly brown hair. He was dressed in a white robe and warrior's outfit with weapons or articles of warfare on his waist and a huge sword. This massive angel had his sword stretched out over the church. The sword must have been at least fifty to sixty foot long!

This astonished me. I had never seen an angel this big before. After the service I couldn't contain myself. I told a pastor there, "Ken, I saw a huge angel step into the church service!" He says, "Are you kidding me?" I responded, "No!" He asked me to describe the angel. It turned out that God had also opened up his spiritual eyes and he saw the same angel. For a moment he thought he might be losing his mind. So when I shared my testimony about seeing the angel, it greatly ministered to him because he also had seen this enormous angel too.

My friends, God has angels like this that have power over entire continents. They have power over cities and regions. I believe that as we learn to co-labor with God's angels, at times God will allow us to loose or activate these mighty angels to actually change the spiritual DNA and the destinies of entire cities, entire regions, entire nations, and even entire continents.

These kinds of angels will play an important part in God's end-time plans for the planet earth. Is it possible that angels like this are an aspect of the powers of the age to come? I believe that God is raising up a group of mature sons and daughters of the Most High God who will be empowered to co-labor with God's angels like the ones that I have just described!

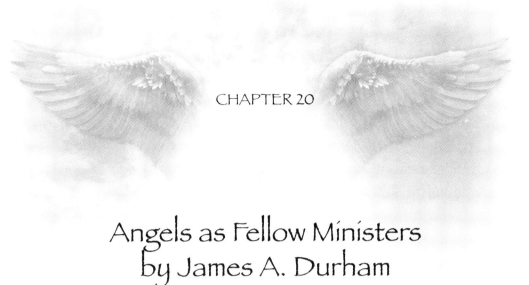

## CHAPTER 20

# Angels as Fellow Ministers by James A. Durham

**Revelation 19:10:**

> *And I fell at his feet to worship him* [an angel]. *But he said to me, "See that you do not do that! I am your fellow servant, and of your brethren who have the testimony of Jesus. Worship God! For the testimony of Jesus is the spirit of prophecy."*

Several years ago as the Lord began to send us on the road more and more for ministry, He began to assign angels to travel with us and minister in the meetings. Each time a new angel was assigned, I would be carried in a vision to a cave where I was introduced to my new ministry partner. One of the first angels to be assigned was a healing angel. I quickly learned something exciting about these angels. They were not alone. They were leaders, and when they manifested a team of angels would come with them. They would suddenly appear in what looked like the huddle of a professional football team. When

I released them to minister, they would quickly move to their assigned individuals and release what the Lord sent them to minister to His people.

An important lesson I learned in the early phases of these assignments was that the Lord and His angels respect our authority. Remember Psalm 115:16: "*The heaven, even the heavens, are the LORD's; But the earth He has given to the children of men.*" In your assigned area, the Lord has given you spiritual authority. It is important to fully grasp what Jesus released to you in Luke 10:19: "*Behold, I give you the authority to trample on serpents and scorpions, and over all the power of the enemy, and nothing shall by any means hurt you.*" The Lord does not capriciously give and then take away your spiritual authority. His angels understand and respect that which has been given to you.

If you want the angels to do more than merely show up, you need to learn to release them to do what Father God send them to do. I recommend that you use care in doing this. Remember 2 Corinthians 11:14-15: "*And no wonder! For Satan himself transforms himself into an angel of light. Therefore it is no great thing if his ministers also transform themselves into ministers of righteousness, whose end will be according to their works.*" Knowing this, we do not want to give legal authority to these counterfeit spirits to release their works. It is important to remember that they are all under the control of a religious spirit and are very legalistic. Therefore, when I perceive the presence of an angel, I always say, "Angel, I release you to minister what Father God sent you to minister." If it is a demon, this gives him no legal authority whatever, because Father God did not send him.

The Lord expects you to do the work of the Kingdom of God in the part of the world assigned to you. Over and over the Lord has decreed: "I give you dominion over the earth and expect you to subdue it and have authority over the birds of the air, the fish of the sea, the beasts of the field and everything that crawls on the face of the earth." (See Genesis 1:28; Psalm 8:6-9.)The really good news is that when we are on our assigned mission in our assigned area, the Lord will provide what we need to get the job done. The angels are released to be ministering spirits with us in order to multiply the outcomes of our work. Remember the teaching in Hebrews 1:14: "*Are they* [angels] *not all ministering spirits sent forth to minister for those who will inherit salvation?*"

We experienced this happening many times during our ministry trips over the years. We have come to expect them to show up and work when released to do so. They were assigned to me for ministry, and I know they will be with me until the Lord cancels their mission. I don't expect that to happen during my lifetime on earth. The Lord is trustworthy and His word is sure. I trust that these angels will always be with us when we are doing His work in ministry.

In addition to the healing angel, the Lord also assigned an angel of protection, an angel of financial breakthrough, an angel of wisdom and revelation, and an angel of holiness to travel with us wherever we go. I have seen them operating so many times, and I call out to them even if I don't see them right away. I summon them to help with the ministry and do the things beyond my abilities. I always expect that healing angel to manifest and work with us in the ministry.

For these and other reasons, we were a little surprised and concerned when my wife, Gloria, had an accident within four hours of our arrival on a ministry trip to South Korea. Both bones in her lower left leg were broken, and the hospital insisted that she needed surgery. We were equally convinced that her leg would be healed in the meetings at church. When it didn't manifest right away, I took it to the heavenly courts and appealed my case to Father God. After my presentation, the Lord spoke to me and made it clear that she was to have the surgery. During the two days of ministry before she returned to the hospital, Gloria prayed for several people who were healed in the meetings. It was confusing at first to see that these people were being healed, but she had to have the surgery.

We later learned that the Lord had other plans for her. He had planned for her to do ministry in the hospital. Many signs, wonders, and healings occurred for others around her in the hospital, and the glory of the Lord was present throughout the time of her hospitalization. Angels manifested in her room and watched over her and ministered with her. She and I were given the opportunity to minister to people who would never have come to our meetings. Buddhists, agnostics, and marginal Christians received ministry and healing and felt the presence of the Holy Spirit and fire. This was her purpose, and she had to pay the price to see the results. She had to have surgery and spend nineteen days in the hospital. But it was all for good because of what the Lord released through her to an unbelieving group of people.

When she did not get healed, it was very disturbing for the pastor of the church. He had been praying and pressing in for several months to have a healing pool like Bethesda in his church. He was expecting to see it happen during our ministry there. He was expecting Gloria to experience a miraculous healing. When she left for the hospital, he was very upset. He had difficulty sleeping and prayed all night for the healing pool to manifest in the church. He shared this with me the next morning, and we came into agreement to change our plans for the ministry that day. Instead of worshipping in the large sanctuary, we gathered in the small chapel downstairs. We had experienced amazing things in this chapel in the past, and we were in faith and agreement that it would happen again. So, we entered into worship with faith and a full expectation for the pool and the anointing to manifest.

Near the conclusion of our worship time, I was given an open vision. I saw an arched stone door standing open on the front right side of the chapel. As I stood looking into this open portal to heaven, I saw water beginning to flow into the worship area and form a pool. I shared this vision with the church, and it was confirmed by other seers. I invited the people to come to the front and form a circle around the pool. We gathered around the area where the water had formed in the spirit. We prayed in the Spirit and made decrees for healing angels to come from heaven and minister to those who needed healing.

As we continued to pray and decree, the healing angel assigned to minister with me manifested and placed the end of his staff in the water and began to stir it around. This was very reminiscent of what happened in the Pool of Bethesda in

Jerusalem. As I shared this, someone shouted that they had been healed. Angels began to manifest one by one; and when we released them to minister what the Lord had sent them to do, others were also getting healed. More and more people gave testimonies of healing.

**John 5:2-4:**

> *Now there is in Jerusalem by the Sheep Gate a pool, which is called in Hebrew, Bethesda, having five porches. In these lay a great multitude of sick people, blind, lame, paralyzed, waiting for the moving of the water. For an angel went down at a certain time into the pool and stirred up the water; then whoever stepped in first, after the stirring of the water, was made well of whatever disease he had.*

Suddenly a new type of angel manifested near the open door. These angels were about three feet tall and hovered as their four wings fluttered rapidly. They actually resembled giant dragonflies and they burned brightly with the fire of the Lord's glory. At first I was fascinated to see something new and just watched them for a short time. Then I remembered my own message about releasing the angels to do what Father God sent them to minister. As I released them, they quickly went to their assigned recipients and released healing fire. As I began to see the angels and to speak of their presence, other seers quickly confirmed they were seeing the same thing.

The pool continued to manifest in each service through-out my time of ministry there. There were more and more testimonies of healings which continued to come in. I am so thankful for what the Lord does for us through His angels. I want to always be able to see them and to know how to minister with them. I want these things for you as well.

**Ephesians 1:3-6:**

> *Blessed be the God and Father of our Lord Jesus Christ, who has blessed us with every spiritual blessing in the heavenly places in Christ, just as He chose us in Him before the foundation of the world, that we should be holy and without blame before Him in love, having predestined us to adoption as sons by Jesus Christ to Himself, according to the good pleasure of His will, to the praise of the glory of His grace, by which He made us accepted in the Beloved.*

Think about it! He has released to you "*every spiritual in the heavenly places in Christ.*" What more could you possibly need? It is not so much a process of receiving these gifts as it is of activating them. Sometimes we need a little jump start to get them going. At times you can just step out in these things as led by the Holy Spirit. At other times you may need for someone to release an impartation and activation.

I want to release an impartation right now for you to begin to minister in these same ways. I want to release an anointing of activation so that you can begin to minister more and more with the angels the Lord is assigning to you. I release to you every anointing and gift the Lord has given to me so that you can minister in the fullness of the blessing. I am asking the Lord to open your spiritual eyes and ears wider than you have ever experienced in the past so that you can more fully discern the things of the Spirit. To complete this impartation, I am praying for you the prayer Paul gave to the church in Ephesus after telling them that they had already received every spiritual blessing. I am doing this because I want you to know that you have already received these spiritual gifts and heavenly blessings in Christ Jesus and to be confident that they can be activated right now.

## Prayer of Activation from Ephesians 1:15-21

*Therefore I also, after I heard of your faith in the Lord Jesus and your love for all the saints, do not cease to give thanks for you, making mention of you in my prayers: that the God of our Lord Jesus Christ, the Father of glory, may give to you the spirit of wisdom and revelation in the knowledge of Him, the eyes of your understanding being enlightened; that you may know what is the hope of His calling, what are the riches of the glory of His inheritance in the saints, and what is the exceeding greatness of His power toward us who believe, according to the working of His mighty power which He worked in Christ when He raised Him from the dead and seated Him at His right hand in the heavenly places, far above all principality and power and might and dominion, and every name that is named, not only in this age but also in that which is to come.*

## CHAPTER 21

# Angels and Milkshakes

My friends, not every angelic encounter has to be as powerful and as fearful as our last testimonies. When I was living in my little house on Beech Street in Bluefield, West Virginia, I would lock myself in the house—sequester myself—and read the word of God, fast and pray, and seek God's face.

It was during this season that God began to open up my spiritual eyes to see angels frequently. During one such season of being sequestered with the Lord, I cut off my television, unplugged my phone, and purposed in my heart I was going to fast and pray until heaven invaded my space. I decided on seven days. I didn't schedule anything. For seven days I purposed in my heart to press into the Kingdom of God and only drink water. So I was on this true fast.

After seventy-two hours the Holy Spirit spoke to me very clearly. He said, "Kevin, I want you to go to Dairy Queen and get a milkshake." I said, "No, Lord. I'm fasting and I'm praying; remember? I want You to open up my eyes to see into the spirit in a greater way. Lord, I want to see Your angels. I know they are here. I can hear them, but I want to see Your angels. So, I'm not going to drink a milkshake; I'm going to do a water fast. I'm going to read, rest, fast, and pray. If You don't come down here, Lord, I'm going to come up there. But I want a breakthrough."

You see, saints, sometimes there are rewards for desperation and determination in the spirit. Jesus said, "*I wish you were…hot…, because you are lukewarm…, I will vomit you out of My mouth*" (Revelation 3:15). So I was pressing into God. Once again the Holy Spirit said, "Kevin, I want you to go to Dairy Queen and get a milkshake." Again I replied, "No, Lord. I'm fasting and praying!"

My friends, it's wise not to argue with the Holy Spirit or to be disobedient, even when He tells us to do simple things that seem foolish. By the way, it is not a good idea to debate with the Holy Spirit. You *cannot* win.

I continued my fast. And about twelve hours later the Holy Spirit said once more, "Kevin, I want you to go to Dairy Queen and get a milkshake." This third time I said, "OK, Lord, but I don't want to end my fast. I want to get a breakthrough; I want to see God's angels."

So, reluctantly I left my little house, walked down Beech Street, and took a left onto the avenue, walking down to Dairy Queen. And as I walked, I began to hear chuckling and laughing. It seemed as if I was being accompanied by a lot of people. But I shrugged that off as I thought that was just my imagination. But the further I walked, the louder the laughter became. It seemed as if the people who were around me were speaking in a foreign language. After a few moments it became very loud and very pronounced. I could hear stones being kicked along the sidewalk. I could hear voices echoing between the buildings as I walked between the buildings on the way to Dairy Queen.

For a moment I was absolutely sure that there were angels who were accompanying me. So I spun around on my left foot as fast as I could and stopped and looked. I suddenly executed a pivot move like a basketball player. And there behind me in a V formation were 144 angels; I'm sure it was 144 angels. They were looking at me and they were jumping up and down; they were waving and they were laughing. God opened my eyes to see those angels. I looked at them for about five or ten seconds. When I blinked my eyes, I couldn't see them anymore; but they were still there. I could still hear them; I could still sense their presence.

I said, "Lord, what do You want me to do?" He said, "Kevin, I want you to go get a milkshake." So I went on to the Dairy Queen and I purchased my milkshake, a chocolate one. As I did that, the angels stood around me. Of course, the other people at the restaurant and the other customers didn't see the angels, but I knew they were there.

As I walked back up the avenue towards the little house on Beech Street, these angels accompanied me. But when I got to the house and turned to go in, I knew the angels were leaving to go to different places, not just in the city but in the region and in the nation. I went back inside, fell down in my prayer closet, and I gave God glory for allowing me to see His angelic host.

My friends, sometimes God will ask us to do things that seem silly in the natural. He will ask you to do an act of obedience. Sometimes these can be peculiar things that seem contrary to what we have purposed in our heart. But obedience, even to do some things like going to get a milkshake when the Holy Spirit tells you to do so, is absolutely critical to activating the eyes of your heart and opening your eyes to see the angels of the Lord that are always around us all. Obedience is critical to activating the gift of discerning of spirits in your life. I also call this ability to see into the spiritual realms or spiritual dimensions the seer anointing. But perhaps chocolate milkshakes are also helpful?

## CHAPTER 22

# Angels in Moravian Falls

Kathy and I currently abide from time to time in Moravian Falls, North Carolina. This is an area where the Moravians, missionaries originally from Germany, prayed and worshiped the Lord continually for 100 years. (I personally believe the prayer furnace was in Germany, but that the Moravians consistently prayed for this area nonetheless. In other words, the hundred years of prayer vigil was not actually done in Moravian Falls, but in Herrnhut, Germany.) Many people have testified that they have encountered angels in the Moravian Falls, North Carolina, area.

Perhaps the Moravian heritage of the area plays a role in the manifestation of the series of "open heavens," spiritual gates, portals, or windows of heaven that are opened in this area? However I believe that it was the prayer and the heritage of the Pentecostal Cherokee Indians that are indigenous to the land that ripped open the heavens with their prayers on the top of the mountains in the Moravian Falls area. But alas, that is the material for another book—*Unlocking the Hidden Mysteries of the Open Heavens of Moravian Falls.*

Some folks around Moravian Falls have been taken into the realms of heavens to receive revelation. Often they are inspired to write about these supernatural encounters that they experience. This is a direct result of the open heavens or spiritual gates in and near Moravian Falls. At times these supernatural encounters reveal the activity of angels. I knew one prophet who refused to sleep in the area because he was constantly receiving too much revelation and supernatural encounters. He said, "I can't get no rest there. The Lord won't let me be."

I am sure that you are aware of the books that have been birthed and written in, or mostly about the Moravian Falls area. If not you may wish to read some of the works of Rick Joyner, Bobby Connor, Gary Oates, or some of the beautiful writings of Anna Rountree. They are all wonderful. Let me take this opportunity to say that there is also a bit of "hype" associated with Moravian Falls, and I deal with that idea in the third book of the trilogy on the seer anointing: *Unlocking the Hidden Mysteries of the Powers of the Age to Come*. Now, allow me to make this highly spiritual and prophetic statement at this point: "Even a blind hog finds a nut every now and again." Think about that (Selah).

## Lay it All Down

At any rate, shortly after Kathy and I completed an extended fast in February 2009, I experienced a powerful prophetic experience in our old ministry office here in Moravian Falls. I had been praying and the Lord spoke to me clearly that it was time to "take the book off the shelf and begin to finish it now." I had begun the manuscript for *The Reality of Angelic Ministry* in 2005. However, after I completed the research and biblical foundation of the book, I hit a wall and was not able to continue with the project while living in Kansas City. So I literally sat the book on a shelf for several years until later in February 2009 when I picked it up again in Moravian Falls. (This was after taking a one year sabbatical from ministry to diligently seek the Lord for the duration of 2008.) Just before I was about to begin to write, the Lord spoke to me very clearly to "take a few minutes and go lay down on the floor in the center of the room."

When I lay down on the pine floor of our old Moravian Falls office, I was immediately "taken up" into the realm of heaven. This experience was very much like the night in Newfoundland when I was translated into the realm of heaven and walked and talked with Jesus all night in the company of angels. During this experience I once again saw the Lord surrounded by the same four angels that I have seen with Him before and Jesus told me that the time had come for the third angel to be assigned to the ministry. The Lord told me this angel's name and explained that this angel was a "scribe angel" and that he would help me to finish the book.

This angel may have been assigned to this geographical area (Moravian Falls). So it is possible that I needed to stop writing until Kathy and I had been obedient to the Spirit to move from Kansas City to Moravian Falls. Again, this is a recurring theme of this book—obedience to the Holy Spirit. Obedience to the Lord is perhaps the most important key to unlocking the ability to discern and see into the heavenly realms in your life. There is no shortcut here. Obedience to the Holy Spirit of God is a supernatural key to activating your ability to see God's angels.

After this experience I wrote almost nonstop for nineteen days in a row, often without any sleep. I would just stop for a few chores or to quickly eat a bite of food. During this time I "knew" that this "scribe angel" was with me in the office. (This was the unction of the Holy Spirit. The leading and/or unction of the Holy Spirit is also an important key to unlocking your ability to discern and "see" into the heavenly realms in your life.) There have been a few occasions that I have seen this angel by an open vision. I saw him waiting for me to come into the office to write one evening. I also I saw him leaning over and looking at the outline that I had taped on the wall beside my desk. The scribe angel pointed with his right index finger at the outline. Instantly I was given supernatural insight, revelation, and direction on how to move forward with the book that I was working on at that time. Much of what you have read to this manuscript has been written since that night in February. In the following section I share the notes that I wrote down after this visitation of Jesus and this specific angelic encounter.

## Journal Notes on Angels in Moravian Falls

*The Lord has just instructed me to open and to begin to record and journal these notes. Today is Friday the 27th of February, 2009. It is 5:03 am. The Spirit instructed me to place what I just written about our conversation tonight in a future book. (I did not believe that it would take another six years for the book to be published!)*

Here is what I wrote that night:

*These last few days have been incredible. Even now I am almost weeping as the presence and goodness of the Lord fill me with awe by what He has done. On February 25, 2009, I had an experience with the Lord. I had been working and trying to write the book The Reality of Angelic Ministry Today. As I started to work in the new ministry offices here in Moravian Falls, the anointing and presence of the Lord began to fill the little office. I began to weep with thankfulness to God for what He has done and is continuing to do in my life. February 25, 2009, was my spiritual birthday, and it appears that my heavenly Father has given me a wonderful supernatural birthday present!*

*My heart is truly being touched and changed as I have been asking the Lord to do a work in my heart according to Psalm 51:10-12: "Create in me a clean heart, O God, And renew a steadfast spirit within me. Do not cast me away from Your presence, And do not take Your Holy Spirit from me. Restore to me the joy of Your salvation, And uphold me by Your generous Spirit." Tonight Papa has answered this "heart prayer" in an amazing way.*

*Tonight the Lord was so very real, so very near, and so very good to me. I am weeping even now as my heart magnifies the Lord. The night of February 25 as I prepared to work on the book, the Lord said to take a minute to lay down on the floor and allow Him to show me some things. When I did the presence and love of Christ invaded my heart, spirit, soul, and body. The Lord spoke to me very clearly. Jesus reminded me of a third heaven experience that I had in 2001. At that time the Lord had promised me that He had four angels that He was assigning to the ministry. At the time I thought this was strange as there was no ministry. It was at that point that this evening, February 25, 2009, I was "taken up" into the realms of heaven. I ascended the hill or into the habitation of God (Psalm 24). (Also see 2 Corinthians 12:3.)*

*During this encounter the Lord assigned a third angel to the ministry. Looking back on these events six years later, I believe that the Father actually gave me a birthday present! This angel has the duty and anointing to "scribe." I had the revelation that this angel would be sent to me at times and would help me as I write. The Lord also told me this morning at about 2:30 a.m. that this angel had been waiting for a long time to be released into the realm of earth to help a saint (believer in Jesus) write. I was very tired as Kathy and I planted six apple trees, two rose bushes, three azalea bushes, and I also planted about seven or eight other pine trees on the edge of the property. I was physically exhausted because I stayed up all night writing on the book on Thursday night. However, I was not able to sleep; so I began to speak to the Lord.*

*The Lord was very near and began to speak to me very clearly and concisely. He told me that since I have set my heart to seek Him that He had drawn near to me, and that His face and countenance was turned towards me too. During the conversation I asked the Lord why I was so physically exhausted but that my mind was so fully awake and why so many thoughts and revelations concerning the book kept coming into my mind. This has happened every night this past week, and I have repeatedly gone up to the office early in the morning between 1 and 3 a.m. to write. The Lord said that the new angel is very near and I am discerning his thoughts as he is preparing to help me write. In fact, the Lord said that he was waiting for me on the steps to the office. When I heard this I got up to go and look for this angel. So when I got out of bed and I walked outside to the office to write this down, it was about 3:20 a.m. (Ephesians 3:20). I saw the angel waiting on the steps of the office as I walked up to write and work on my personal computer.*

*When I rounded the corner this angel was apparently very glad to see me and appeared to be anxious to "get to work." He was smiling and rubbing both hands together in an excited manner. I stopped short of the first step and smiled at him too. He was wearing a beautiful white robe, which was giving off a translucent glow or phosphorescence. It emitted enough heavenly light that I could make out this angel's countenance. It was then that I realized that this was one of the four angels that*

*Jesus had introduced me to in the heavenly realms back in 2001. In fact, this angel has on occasion held me up by my right arm and right hand in the heavenly realms. This angel is a friend of mine, and a member of God's heavenly family to which I have been engrafted. He seemed very glad to see me again, and I must admit that the feeling was mutual. He turned and bounded up the stairs to the office with me right on his heels. It was time to go to work! However, I knew that it was also time to pray.*

When I entered the office I no longer had an open vision of this heavenly visitor who had come to co-labor with me and to help me in writing books. However, I was able to discern his presence and the atmosphere of the office was charged with the fragrance and atmosphere of heaven. Pure joy and a radical faith bubbled up from within my spirit and I understood that I needed to dialog with the Lord Jesus and I bowed my knees to the Father of Lights (James 1:17). I placed my knees on the knotty pine floor with my elbows on the soft material of my old brown recliner that I had kept in my prayer room in Kansas City. I had been taken to heaven in that chair to sit with Jesus in the heavenly places in 2006. As my elbows touched the material of my faithful companion (this brown rocking chair), the glory of God exploded into my spirit in a new and fantastic way. The Lord began to speak to me and gave me some personal revelation about this scribe angel and the others. The Lord instructed me to write it down. That is why I can share it with you in this book.

Here is what the Lord spoke to me about the three angels that He has assigned to my life and the ministry. These heavenly experiences first started in 2001 before I traveled to Newfoundland. In the little house at 121 Beech Street I had a lot of heavenly encounters. As you will recall from a previous testimony, in one such encounter I saw Jesus motion to me to come into His presence and I was taken into the realms of heaven whilst I was fasting and praying to Him. When I arrived the Lord was flanked by four angels. It was then that the Lord told me that he was going to assign those four angels to my life and the ministry.

He assigned one soon after that. He assigned one more angel to me about ten months later in Canada. The third He assigned on the night of February 25, 2009. There is still a fourth that was assigned at a later time on April 29, 2012, at our little cabin in Moravian Falls, North Carolina. This particular angel is one of God's mighty angels of creative miracles and supernatural provision. I will share that amazing testimony in volume #2 of *Modern Day Testimonies of Angelic Encounters and Other Supernatural Experiences*. But getting back this testimony from February 25, 2009, allow me to conclude that testimony in the following chapter.

## CHAPTER 23

# The Character of God's Angels

My journal continues:

*Tonight as I was praying in my office I had a wonderfully clear and direct dialog and conversation with the Lord Jesus about the four angels that He had promised to assign to the ministry. As we spoke the Lord told about these first three angels. And the Lord seemed to be truly elated that I was able to believe, receive, and walk in these supernatural dynamics of His Kingdom. The first angel of God was assigned to help protect me and also to provide provision. I was also instructed on how and why I could release the angel of provision to accomplish a specific task. The results have been very miraculous when I have been allowed and instructed to employ this angel. (This was the first angel that the Lord assigned at the little house on Beech Street and I have been allowed and released to co-labor with this angel many, many times over the years.)*

*This angel's personality is much like the first Adam. He is not the first Adam but has a character a similar personality like the first Adam. Let me be clear on this. The first Adam was given authority over the earth. He was anointed to be fruitful and to multiply (he was anointed to provide provision and act in the role or anointing of a care taker, overseer, or guardian). The first Adam had authority over the earth and its provision. This angel also has that type of anointing and can at times act on an individual's behalf in this manner (to release protection or provision). The first Adam was to be a caretaker or protector of the earth and all that was in it. God had given the first Adam dominion over the earth or the role of protector.*

We see this in Genesis 1:26-31:

*Then God said, "Let Us make man in Our image, according to Our likeness; let them have dominion over the fish of the sea, over the birds of the air, and over the cattle, over all the earth and over every creeping thing that creeps on the earth." So God created man in His own image; in the image of God He created him; male and female He created them. Then God blessed them, and God said to them, "Be fruitful and multiply; fill the earth and subdue it; have dominion over the fish of the sea, over the birds of the air, and over every living thing that moves on the earth." And God said, "See, I have given you every herb that yields seed which is on the face of all the earth, and every tree whose fruit yields seed; to you it shall be for food. Also, to every beast of the earth, to every bird of the air, and to everything that creeps on the earth, in which there is life, I have given every green herb for food"; and it was so. Then God saw everything that He had made, and indeed it was very good. So the evening and the morning were the sixth day.*

The original Adam was given authority over the earth. Please understand that the Lord was giving me further revelation and understanding of His angels and their nature by showing me this angel's character or characteristics in certain passages of scripture. I am not implying that these angels referred to here are the people depicted in the Scripture, but that their behavior is similar to people written about in the Bible only.

## Assignment of Angels

*The second angel that Jesus assigned was named \_\_\_\_. (I will not record or share these angels' names.) This angel was assigned to me in Botwood, Newfoundland, Canada, in November 2001. His role was to minister for people (Hebrews 1:14). His personality and anointing is similar to that of Moses' brother Aaron who helped the people to overcome and be cleansed from their sins. Of course, this is a foreshadow of the ministry of Jesus. Nonetheless, Moses' brother Aaron was anointed to minister unto the Lord and to intercede on behalf of the people. The role of Jesus was to give total salvation—spirit, soul, and body. So we could say that Moses' brother Aaron ministered as a type of Christ. God's angels also work or co-labor with* *us human beings (weird spiritual creatures) at times to help us recreate Christ in our sphere of influence. God's angels cannot release salvation, but the Lord can use His angels to draw people closer to Jesus as Savior.*

*The second angel also has a personality or character similar to that of the Moses' brother Aaron. The Lord showed me that this second angel stands behind me at times as I minister or pray for the sick. There have been times when I have seen this angel and have realized in the past. This angel is a type of "healing angel." However, tonight I had a knowing that this angel releases a glory and anointing of the Spirit of the Lord that is much more than just healing of the sick. It is possible that he is also used to help us to know how to "speak a word in season" or to release a prophetic word of exhortation or edification. This is the kind of angelic ministry that is revealed or outlined in Isaiah 50, verse 4, and is a model for this type of biblical principle; "The Lord GOD has given Me The tongue of the learned, that I should know how to speak A word in season to him who is weary. He awakens Me morning by morning, He awakens My ear To hear as the learned."*

*There are times when this specific angel stands behind me and whispers into my left ear as I minister to people. It is easy for me to simply repeat the secrets of men and women's hearts as the angel reveals them to me. I should also point out that the anointing of the Holy Spirit is also very active when this healing angels manifests. This angel will also at times whisper to me and tell me when people are speaking lies or have nefarious plans or agendas. Usually, I will not tell them that I have this knowledge. I just allow them to continue on with their ways.*

*Inevitably, the truth is revealed and God triumphs in these instances. Many times when this specific angel stands behind me I will be told or I will have a word of wisdom and I will know the thoughts or intents or people's hearts (good and bad) and often will be given revelation of their sin issues when I look into their eyes (smile). I usually don't let them know; I just intercede for them or address the sin in the manner that the Holy Spirit directs me. I have led a lot of people to the Lord Jesus as Savior in this way, by telling them the secrets of their hearts and sharing the goodness and love of Jesus with them.*

*Whatever the other anointing and duties assigned to this second angel may be, he is certainly used to help me or to co-labor with me as I minister to the saints. This angel helps to release physical healing to people's bodies, he is involved in releasing emotional healing to people's souls, and finally he is also used to help set people free from demonic oppression (deliverance). This angel is used to help release miracles and healings. In fact, when this particular angel shows up there are often creative miracles that manifest. One example of this would be when a man named Leonard grew an entire new eyeball in the nation of Malawi over the course of five days. (This is a very well documented creative miracle.) Hebrews 1:14 speaks of these duties of God's angels: "Are they not all ministering spirits [angels] sent forth to minister for those who will inherit salvation?"*

The point is that God assigns individual angels duties and assignments upon the earth. God's angels are always busy attending to their duties and heeding the word of the Lord.

## Scribe Angels

*The angel that the Lord assigned to me on the 25th is named ____. This is the angel that I saw as the Lord spoke to me that night saying that this angel's duty was as a "scribe" angel. I do not have all of the revelation or understanding this aspect of angelic ministry; but is clear from scripture that there is a lot of writing done in heaven, and I assume that it is angels that are employed to do it. I call these scribe angels.*

*The Lord told me that even as the healing angel stands behind me as I pray and minister that this third angel would stand behind me as I write (what the Spirit of the Lord directs me to write). I am not certain, but there is also the thought or possibility that this angel is linked or has an association, relationship, or connection to Moravian Falls. The Lord told me those things on the night that the angel was in the office the first time.*

*Jesus also reminded me of the very first time I flew into MCI airport in Kansas City in August 2001. The Holy Spirit told me, "You need to get used to this." At that moment I had a revelation that I would be flying in and out of MCI and Kansas City a lot. This was before I had any intention or idea that I was to move to KC. About three years later as I would fly into or fly out of the airport once or twice nearly every month, the Holy Spirit would always remind me of that unlikely (in the natural) promise dozens of times over the next five or more years. Even today I fly into and out of Kansas City International Airport frequently. I always just smile and be reminded of the goodness and faithfulness of the Lord to perform His word. It is Isaiah 55:11 manifest in my life: "So shall My word be that goes forth from My mouth; It shall not return to Me void, But it shall accomplish what I please, And it shall prosper in the thing for which I sent it." So again, the third angel that Jesus assigned to me was the scribe angel that I have mentioned earlier.*

*In this same manner the Lord told me that I was to get used to writing here in the ministry offices in Moravian Falls. I have a "knowing" this is a "word" like the one from 2001 about the airport in Kansas City (MCI). Again I do not have all the revelation about the aspects of this "scribe angel," but I trust in the Lord. (As of this writing I have finished ten books in Moravian Falls.)*

*I do know that there are a lot of books in heaven according to Malachi 3:16 and also because of a third heaven experience that I had where two angels took me to the library where Jesus was sitting and waiting for me.*

*In that experience I saw a vault or libraries where there were literally millions upon millions of books. There were also millions and millions of ancient scrolls stored and cataloged very carefully in the Father's library. I was guided by the two angels (at the direction of Jesus) to enter. There I found the Book of the Life of my youngest daughter. I began to read it, but I was overcome with emotion and stopped after I got to the point where she was six years old. However, I know that God has a plan for her life and I still take great comfort in that fact to this day.*

*That is all for now, but here are several scriptures in connection with scribe angels, books, scrolls, and other writings in the realms of heaven. The key verse that the Lord gave me tonight was that of Malachi 3:16: "Then those who feared the LORD spoke to one another, And the LORD listened and heard them; So a book of remembrance was written before Him For those who fear the LORD And who meditate on His name." I believe that angels like I have described here scribe these heavenly books of remembrance in the realms of heaven.*

Here are several other scriptures that the Lord birthed in my heart concerning "scribe angels," and my call to write this book, and possibly others as well: Psalm 40:7; Psalm 69:28; Psalm 139:16; Jeremiah 30:1; and Jeremiah 36. I also believe that the Lord of Glory, the Lord of Hosts, has angels like the ones described in the previous two chapters that can be released to co-labor with you to help you recreate Christ in your sphere of influence. The question becomes: can you believe to receive it?

# CHAPTER 24

# The Angel of the Lord

In 2006 Kathy and I had the opportunity to travel to India to conduct a soul-winning outreach. We were ministering in a large city on the eastern part of India. God was doing some wonderful things. There was a lot of warfare on those meetings. To be honest, I was a bit disappointed even though we were seeing miracles and we were seeing people saved; we just weren't seeing as many salvations as I had hoped for.

I must admit that India was one of the most difficult places that I have ever sought to preach in crusade ministry. I was actually physically assaulted while I preached almost every night. On that last night of the crusade, it felt as if I had been punched or stabbed in the stomach as I gave the altar call for salvation. (When I returned to the USA, it appeared that I had developed a hernia. I never accepted this diagnosis; however, I did have the symptoms for over three years until I was sovereignly healed in the spring of 2009.) I preached for several nights and there was little fruit from the meetings and only about 1500 people had answered the call for salvation even though there had been dozens of healings and notable miracles in the meetings.

I was asked to speak at a very large church on Sunday morning and was told that there would be about 20,000 in the service. I was told by the church leadership that I was to perform miracles, and that I could not do any altar calls. I was instructed that I could not step off the platform nor could I wear my shoes on the platform. I was not to take any testimonies from those who were healed. They told me, "You have forty minutes to preach. You can work miracles for eight minutes." So I thought, "Lord, I'm going to need your help." And by the way, I had to stop speaking at 10:50 and I was to perform all the miracles before 10:58 because they had to have Sunday school meetings then. All of this information was told to me about twenty minutes before the service. I was also told that the pastor of the church would not be attending the "miracle service" because he was suffering from a sore throat.

As I sat on the platform that morning in the midst of the other forty pastors from the church, I was truly astonished to see about 19,000 people in attendance. They had opened the sides of the building and had set up tents on the sides. To be honest, I do not think I was a welcome speaker by some of the clergy. I remembered that the Lord has said that He would meet me in India, but up to that point He was nowhere in sight and I was beginning to think that I had missed the Lord by coming. What would transpire next forever changed my life.

I began to preach on faith, the currency of Christ, and the total salvation Jesus bought for us on the Cross of Calvary. I was looking at the clock as I knew I did not have much time, and the interpreter seemed to take about three minutes to repeat every sentence I was preaching. At about the same moment that these thoughts entered my mind, I heard a funny sound coming from behind me on the platform where the forty pastors were sitting. While the interpreter was relaying my last sentence, I turned around to find the source of the sounds. I was a little astonished to see that a handful of the pastors had actually fallen asleep and were snoring. At that instant I let out a heart's cry of prayer to the Lord: "Oh precious Holy Spirit, I need your help! Lord, I'm not getting through. I need your help here!" I noticed that a strong breeze began to blow into the church and ruffled the tents on the side of the meeting at that moment.

I worked the sermon and sought to finish a little early with the thought of giving the Lord a little more time than eight minutes to work miracles. Something began to stir in my spirit and a Holy desperation began to pour out from me. Surely among all of the thousands of people who were present, there were many who needed healing. But I would only have eight more minutes to see the Lord touch all of the 19,000 or so on hand.

## Preach Salvation

With the grace of the Lord, I finished the preaching and had an extra three minutes to work the miracles. You may be thinking, why didn't you just move directly into healing and not preach the sermon? That is a good question; and the answer is that I was seeking to be obedient to the Lord as possible. The Holy Spirit had clearly told me to preach to the people about faith and salvation. When I finished I told the people over the snores of the pastors that I was going to ask the Lord Jesus to come and release healing to everyone. I quickly told the people to place their hands of the part of their bodies that needed a miracle.

I said, "If you have a tumor, put your hand on your tumor. If you have a blind eye, put your hand on your blind eye. If you have a bad back, touch your back. If you are deaf or have a deaf friend, place your fingers in the deaf ear. If you have a special need from God, silently pray and ask Jesus to meet you at your point of need." I then asked everyone to bow their heads and close their eyes; I asked that anyone who was not sure if they were saved to pray a prayer of salvation with me.

"Oh, Jesus won't You come and help me this morning," I began to think as the interpreter rambled on. A moment later I saw a blinding flash of light in the back of the congregation. I felt the power of God come. It was a Luke 5:17 situation. I knew the power of God was present to heal. When I looked into the back left corner where I had seen the bright flash of light, I saw Jesus! This was an open eyed vision of the Lord. Jesus had literally stepped into the church. When He did, the power of God came in an unusually strong and tangible way that I have rarely experienced.

When this happened I saw what I can only describe as an explosion of light in the far back left side of the church, and immediately I was aware that the power of God had just entered the church and the Lord was about to do something spectacular! Unexpectedly, my body burst into a series of pains and symptoms of sickness. The first thing that happened was that I went blind for a second or two, and I began to declare:

"Jesus is here to heal blind eyes!" When I said this there was screams that seemed to come from the back corner where I had seen the blast of light.

When my vision returned and I looked back in that corner of the church, I saw the Angel of the Lord! I saw Jesus step into the sanctuary! He was wearing a white robe and a talite with blue and gold trim over His head. Jesus was walking from the back left corner of the church towards the platform! I could see that the Lord was touching people on the heads. And as He touched the people, many would faint or scream. I kept feeling explosions of pains, or what some call "empathetic words of knowledge," shooting through my body. Each time I felt a symptom, I would call it out; and it seemed that healings and miracles were exploding throughout the church. People began to scream and fall over. I no longer waited for the interpreter to catch my words, as I knew that the Lord was now moving sovereignly in our midst. (See John 5:17.)

I continued to watch as Jesus slowly walked through the entire crowd of about 19,000 touching various individuals. Jesus walked from my left to the right. When He got to the middle of the crowd, He turned His direction a little and walked right to the right hand corner of the church touching people every step of the way. I continued to call out healing after healing. It seemed that as Jesus touched each person, I had a "knowing" of what He was doing and would simply declare the healing. People began to scream, as the Lord Jesus was walking through the congregation. I could see that as the Lord walked through, He would touch people. And as He would touch people, I knew that miracles were happening. I simply began to minister in the gift of the word of knowledge. I call out the miracle after miracle and healing after healing: "Someone's tumor just dissolved!" "Someone's blind eye is opening!" "Part of someone's foot just grew back." "Someone's spine is being regenerated." "Someone's foot is growing; several deaf ears just popped open; a tumor on the breast just dissolved; several people with skin conditions are being cleansed; another blind eye just opened." God was doing amazing miracles, and the Kingdom had come! I went on, and on like this for about eight minutes.

CHAPTER 25

# The Eyes of the Messiah

When Jesus reached a place near the front right side of the platform, He stopped for a moment and turned to the platform. Jesus smiled at me and continued to touch people and people continued to be healed. It was such a sweet smile. In an instant I remembered His words to me in Newfoundland and in Tanzania: "I am going to open the nations to you and you will preach My word with power, and Lo I will be with you always." For just a split second I wanted to jump down and run to fall at the Lord's feet, but I knew that He wanted me to minister to the people.

I was crying, and I was in a state of ecstasy in the same instant! At that moment I saw a young boy about six years old run up to Jesus; he was looking up into the eyes of the Messiah. Jesus smiled at the lad. He reached out with His right hand, and He touched him on top of the boy's head. And then I watched as Jesus walked to the corner of the church and simply vanished.

By now people all over the church were standing and falling and weeping and all sorts of commotions were taking place, except behind me on the platform where several of the pastors continued to sleep soundly and snore. I looked at the clock and estimated that Jesus had been in the church for exactly eight minutes. I have often wondered what would have happened if the leadership would have allotted more than "eight minutes to work miracles"? I asked for everyone to sit down and to listen to me carefully.

I told them if they had been healed to stand to their feet. To my amazement about 17,000 people stood up. I told the people to sit back down and listen to me very carefully. I said; "Only stand up if you are 100 percent certain that you have been healed of your sickness. If your tumor is gone, check for the tumor. Check your deaf ear, check your blind eye; make sure that you are hearing and seeing. Check your bad back. Check to see if your fingers or toes or feet actually grew back. Make sure that are certain that you are healed. If you are sure that you have been healed, stand to your feet." Again about 15,000 people stood up!

Again I told the congregation to sit back down and listen to me very, very carefully: "Only stand up if you are 100 percent certain that you have been healed of your sickness. If your tumor is gone, check for the tumor. Check your deaf ear, check your blind eye; make sure that you are hearing and seeing. Check your bad back. Check to see if your fingers or toes or feet actually grew back. Make sure that are certain that you are healed. If you are sure that you have been healed, stand to your feet. Do not stand up unless you are 100 percent sure that you can prove you have been healed." This time about 12,000 people stood to their feet! I said, "Let's give Jesus Christ a great shout of praise for the healings He has just done!" The congregation with one accord lifted up a mighty shout and praise to the Lord. It seemed at that moment that the earth literally shook. The praise lasted for about two minutes until I asked them to stop shouting and praising the Lord. (I only had two minutes left before Sunday school was due to start.)

I pivoted supernaturally on my right foot like a spinning top and began to point at each pastor on the platform in turn. By now they had been aroused from their slumber and were wondering what on earth was happening? I went down the row and told the people who had been healed, all 12,000 or so, to come to the pastors in person and to tell the pastors exactly what Jesus had just done for them, to give their testimonies. The pastors were all now wide-eyed and did not know what to think. It turned out that each pastor had several hundred people who they were responsible to oversee and shepherd, so it seemed that this last minute plan to glorify Jesus for His miracles would work out great.

My time was up! I walked off the platform and motioned to the driver to take me to the hotel. I wanted to fall on my face and praise the Lord privately, giving Him thanks for the mighty miracles He did in the church that morning. I invested the rest of the morning praising God. Kathy and I told our guests that we wanted to rest the next day and did not wish to be disturbed. The host pastor continued to call about every two or three hours. He was very excited. The people had begun to come to the pastors immediately after the service, as I had asked, to report their healings. The pastors were astonished. The host pastor would call and report another powerful miracle about every two hours.

## Totally Healed

Later that night he told me that many people who were blind were healed. I asked, "You mean people who wore glasses or do you mean people were totally blind." He said; "Brother Kevin, I mean that they were totally blind; there are many blind that were healed." I asked the pastor how he knew; and he said that they are coming to give the pastors the testimonies. He said that the blind all sat in the back corner of the church together and many were healed. I asked; "Which corner did the blind sit in?" The host pastor said, "In the back left corner from the platform."

That was the place I had seen the Lord Jesus step into the room. The host pastor went on: "Brother Kevin, the pastors are amazed! There are hundreds of people coming to them giving all kinds of testimonies. There are deaf who can hear. Part of one man's foot grew back. Another woman who is a famous singer has had her back healed; she has had serious back surgery but she is totally healed. Many tumors have disappeared. And the people are still coming to the pastors. They have been coming all day. We need to get all of these testimonies." I laughed and told him thanks; we decided to have lunch the next day before we flew out to Goa.

The Lord in His sovereignty had met me at my point of weakness; and in my weakness His strength was made perfect (2 Corinthians 12:9). Kathy and I flew to Goa for a much needed rest, as we had been traveling extensively that year and wanted to take a break before we got back on another airplane for an international flight.

We checked into our hotel in Goa and decided to take a walk by the ocean. It was a beautiful sunny day and we enjoyed each other's company. We were also talking about the fantastic miracles and healings the Lord had done the past Sunday. It still boggles my mind. We enjoyed our stroll and stopped to have a cool refreshing drink in the restaurant before returning to the room. When we walked into the room, the phone rang almost immediately. I looked at Kathy and shrugged saying, "Who on earth could that be?"

I answered the phone, and it was the host pastor! He was very excited and said, "Brother Kevin, you must come back! The pastors all want you to come back now. The Lord has done marvelous things! They are all astonished. The people have continued to come and they are still getting the testimonies every day. They really want you to come back." Again I chuckled at him and asked when they wanted us to come back. The host pastor said, "Now! They want you to come back right now!" I told the host pastor that we could not come back so quickly. In hindsight I wonder if perhaps we should have cancelled our reservations and returned. But Kathy and I both felt the mission in that city had been completed when the Angel of the Lord appeared. After a few too short days we returned home to Kansas City.

You see, my friends, Jesus still steps into our miracle services today as well. I want you to know something. Jesus still continues to visit our churches today. At times He comes as Jehovah Rapha; Jesus comes as the God who heals you. And when Jesus comes, He often comes with His angelic host as the King of kings and the Lord of lords. I give Him all of the glory for the miracles we saw in India. And I believe God wants to do those same kinds of miracles everywhere, everywhere in the world; not just in third-world nations, but in America, Canada, Australia, France, Indonesia, China, Great Britain, and in every nation upon the earth. Learn to expect the unexpected! The Kingdom of God is at hand! The Angel of the Lord is on the move!

## CHAPTER 26

# Angels Miracles, Signs and Wonders

In 2005 Kathy and I had been invited to the city of Hoogeveen in the Netherlands to speak at a Miracles, Signs, and Wonders Conference. We'd been invited by Tabernacle Ministries. We were going to minister with a man named Jaap Dieleman, who was a well-known healing evangelist in the Netherlands.

They had asked me to speak first at the signs and wonders conference, so I had been praying and asking the Lord, "What do You want me to speak about? How do I open a Miracles, Signs, and Wonders Conference in Holland?" Holland can be a bit of a difficult place to minister in because there is an air of unbelief that is prominent among some of the people. The Lord began to speak to me that He wanted me to preach from Luke chapter 3. I said, "OK, Lord." That seemed very appropriate; a great way to start a miracles, signs, and wonders event.

The day the conference was to start was beautiful. When I arrived at the church, it was a crisp, clear fall day, with beautiful sunshine, blue skies, and fresh air. I walked into the church where the conference was being held. It was a beautiful old edifice, hundreds of years old. It was an old stone building with massive stained glass windows. I thought, "This is a beautiful church!" But it was full of doubt; it was full of unbelief because it was a denominational church that had cessationist theology. They didn't believe in miracles; they didn't believe in healing; they didn't believe in the gifts of the Spirit. They thought those all ceased with the original twelve apostles. I thought this odd. But it seemed that the church was going to garner a profit from renting the building out to our hosts for a miracles, signs, and wonders event.

So I thought, "It's odd that we are having a signs and wonders conference here." But, nonetheless, it was beautiful! As the early sun shone through the stained glass windows, the sanctuary of that edifice was filled with a beautiful blue light. I thought, "This is really nice." These windows were massive; they were about fifty feet tall and perhaps twenty to twenty-five feet wide. As the brilliant sunlight filtered through the designs in the stained glass, it gave a kind of ethereal feel to the sanctuary.

When my time came to speak, I stepped up to the podium. As I opened my Bible and laid it down, it supernaturally fell open to the Book of Luke chapter 3. I began to read about how Jesus was baptized and the Holy Spirit appeared bodily in the form of a dove (vv. 21-22). As I spoke those words, out of the corner of my eye I saw a shadow outside. I looked to my left, and I saw the shadow of a bird that was heading directly toward this huge stained glass window to my left. In my heart I thought, "Lord, that bird is going to crash into the window!"

At that moment the bird burst through the window, but not in the natural. The bird supernaturally came through the glass; and there in front of me was the most beautiful iridescent dove I've ever seen. It began to flutter its wings and hover in one place. The beautiful blue color of its pinfeathers sort of radiated and there was a powerful explosion of glory that came from this supernatural dove. I was astonished! I stopped speaking and stared at this dove as it hovered in one place for several seconds.

As it came through the window, as this dove manifested, the power and glory of the Holy Spirit exploded in the sanctuary. And, once again it was Luke 5:17; I knew that the power of God was present to heal. And I could feel a multitude of angels come into the church. The Lord had spoken to me previously and said, "When you feel the healing angels come, I want you to pray for the deaf."

I stared at the supernatural dove. Suddenly it took off and it flew in my direction and it flew behind my head. I spun around, and as I watched it disappeared in the corner of the church. Just poof, it was gone! I was astonished. I was silent. By now twenty or thirty seconds had passed since I had said anything. I had forgotten where I was. I looked at the people who were in the conference and asked, "Did anybody just see that?" Maybe 20 percent of the people put their hands up. Dozens of people had seen the Holy Spirit descend at the Miracles, Signs, and Wonders Conference bodily in the form of a dove. I thought, "Praise God! We have just seen our first sign and wonder."

I called for the deaf, as the Holy Spirit had instructed me. Two women came forward. They appeared to be African. They were both deaf. One woman was totally deaf from birth, forty-seven years. The other woman was deaf in one ear; she had been deaf for thirty-seven years. As I prayed for the second woman, her deaf ear opened. She began to give God glory as we prayed for the totally deaf woman. Her ears also opened. They began to hug each other and weep and cry. As I tried to get their testimony, it was difficult; but they shared their testimony of how they had just been healed. One woman said the Lord had spoken to her and said, "If you'll go to the Miracles, Signs, and Wonders Conference, I'll give you the miracle for the healing of your deaf ear." And she received her healing that day. She was from Ghana, South America. I give God all the glory for healing these deaf women.

## Gorredijk

You see, saints, sometimes God still does signs and wonders. Sometimes the Holy Spirit still comes bodily in the form of a dove. And when the Holy Spirit comes, the heavens open. And when the heavens open, God's angels come to minister for those who inherit salvation. Two years later I was speaking in Gorredijk and I was sharing the testimony of how the dove came to the Miracles, Signs, and Wonders Conference. I said, "Is there anybody here today that was in that meeting two years ago?" A woman came forward and gave her testimony. Here's what she said, "Kevin, I had gone to that meeting when I was ready to walk away from God. My heart was hardened. I said, 'God I'm going to this meeting, this supposed so-called Miracles, Signs, and Wonders Conference. And if you don't show me Yourself, if You don't give me a sign, I'm turning away from God. I'm turning away from Jesus and I'm going back into the world.'"

She continued, "That day you came to me and you gave me a testimony of how God had delivered you from drugs. You were giving away your CDs, and you asked if anyone had a son or a daughter who was addicted to drugs. I raised my hand because my son was on heroin. You came and you handed me the CD and you turned away. But as you turned away, you turned back to me and you said, 'Your son will be saved within one year. God will do a miracle in his life.' You said it so gently but with such power that I just believed what you had said. I was thinking about that when you said for everyone to open their Bibles. And that's when I saw the dove. I saw that dove you are talking about, Kevin. It did come through the window. And the second that dove appeared, God spoke to me and I heard His voice for the first time in years. He said, 'Will you still leave Me now?'"

She said, "I rededicated my life to Jesus that day. I took that CD and I gave it to my son. He didn't take it at first, but then he took it. He listened to your CD and he prayed the prayer of salvation at the end. He was delivered from heroin in one or two days. Today he is going to ministerial school and he wants to be a youth pastor." Praise Jesus for that!

Saints, you see, sometimes when the Holy Spirit comes, the heavens open over our lives. We need to have an understanding and revelation about the importance of open heavens. And, my friends, when you can get the heavens opened over your life, you'll begin to see God's angels. But more importantly than that, you'll have communion and *koinonia* with the Holy Spirit. And when you are in relationship with the Spirit of God,

He will show you through the unction of the Spirit of God how to co-labor with God's angels just like I shared in this last testimony. This can transform your life. It can transform who you are, from an ordinary person and a regular believer in Jesus to an overcomer who can manifest Christ's Kingdom upon the earth with accompanying miracles, signs and wonders.

## Prayer of Thanks Giving

*Father, in the name of Jesus, I thank You for everyone who has read these testimonies. And, God, I thank You that the testimony of Jesus Christ is the spirit of prophecy. Lord, I pray for those who have it upon their hearts to step into Your Kingdom, God; to inherit Your Kingdom, God; to taste Your Kingdom, O Lord; to see Your Kingdom, Jesus; that You would open up the eyes of their hearts and that they could begin to see that those who are for us are more than those who are against us, and that greater is He who is in them and greater is He who is in me than the one who is in the world. And, Father, we thank You for the blood of Jesus; we thank You for the atonement of the cross and the finished work that Jesus did there. Lord, thank You for Your shed blood which covers our sins and the stripes You took upon Your back for the healing of our bodies. And, Lord, we give You all praise, all honor, and all glory for everything You've done and every testimony that I've shared in this book. May You alone receive the glory. In Jesus' mighty name I pray. Amen.*

## CHAPTER 27

# Angel in the Combat Zone

In 2006 I experienced one of the most powerful and memorable visitations of an angel that I have ever encountered. This is great example of how God can use an angel to give direction. During this angelic encounter I was not alone in the room when the angel appeared. At that time I was traveling with a bishop from Tanzania. The bishop and I were in Entebbe, Uganda, on the way to Gulu, Uganda. Our mission was to learn more about the orphanage ministry. We had also carried along with us our battery powered bullhorns in hopes of preaching in the refugee camp at Pabo, Uganda. Pabo is considered to be one of the largest and most destitute PDC (People Displacement Camps) in the entire world.

My good friend Duncan Hill is the founder of the Uganda Orphans Fund, and we were traveling as his guests. Duncan has produced a great video about the plight of the children in the Gulu region called *Cry of the Bush*. I strongly encourage you to watch that video on the internet if you would like to have more insight to the problems the children face in the region.

There were at that time up to tens of thousands of people who had fled to Pabo in an attempt to avoid the atrocities of the Lord's Resistance Army. The Lord's Resistance Army is a terrorist organization that has been persecuting and terrorizing the peoples of northern Uganda and Sudan for years. The LRA's alleged tactics include kidnapping innocent children. It has been reported that the LRA has forced the boys, from ages five to thirteen, to murder their families or to be killed. If they do kill the members of the family, they are indoctrinated into the LRA. We were given first-hand testimonies from individuals who had escaped that this involves a series of blood oaths and secret ceremonies. It was reported to us that once the children are indoctrinated, they become cold, hardhearted killers who take their orders from the LRA leadership. However, Uganda Orphans Fund is seeking to rescue and liberate these children that are abducted by the LRA.

It is common knowledge that the LRA also kidnaps the little girls when they raid villages looking to increase the numbers of their ranks. These little girls can be as young as five to eight and up to eighteen. Once the girls are kidnapped, they are forced to become wives of child soldiers or the officers of the LRA. Because of the genocide in the region, there are a multitude of orphans in the area. These child brides often are orphaned themselves. Once they become pregnant, it has been reported that, they are often murdered. Therefore, many of the girls seek escape when they find that they are with child to avoid death and to bear their child. This is doubly complicated because the orphaned girl gives birth to an orphaned child.

We were staying in the Imperial Botanical Beach Hotel in room 25, in Entebbe. We were to be working with my friend, who is building children's homes in the Gulu region. The children from the surrounding areas flock to Gulu every night in the attempt to avoid being kidnapped or murdered. They are called children of the night. It was not uncommon at that time to see thousands of children pour into Gulu in the evenings. Many would have walked miles to reach the relative safety of Gulu. They sleep in temporary camps and many simply sleep in the streets. This humanitarian crisis has been mostly ignored by the Western world.

We had high expectations for this trip, and we hoped to learn more about building orphanages and helping the children. Our trip had been coincidentally timed to fall within a short-lived cease-fire between the Ugandan Army and the LRA. There were representatives from NATO, WHO, and other international organizations in Gulu in hope of brokering a lasting peace with the LRA to end the genocide and violence. The area is dangerous; some foreigners and journalists had been kidnapped and killed in the region. There is also the threat of unexploded land mines which litter the region around Gulu and Pabo.

## A Light from Heaven

The bishop and I had enjoyed a good dinner and were settling into our nice room at the Imperial Botanical Beach Hotel. There was a bit of a nervous tension in the air, and we were both a little uneasy to be traveling into a war zone even with the shaky cease-fire still in effect. We both fell into an uneasy sleep about 10 p.m. after we had prayed together asking the Lord for protection, wisdom, and direction for the trip into the Gulu region. About 2 a.m. I was jolted awake by the power and presence of the Lord. I sat up in the bed, and the fear of the Lord was hanging thickly in the room. There was also a bright light that was hurting my eyes.

My first thought was to be a little aggravated with the bishop. It was late. What on earth was he doing with the light on? Suddenly I realized that the lamp was not on. I looked up into the corner of the room and there was a large ball of lightning hovering. The ball of light was about eighteen inches in circumference, and it was slightly moving up and down as it hovered about ten feet in the air. Suddenly I had the revelation that this was one of God's angels that was visiting us. Every hair on my body stood on end, and the fear of a Holy God flooded my spirit, soul, and body. I quickly glanced to my right to see what the bishop was doing.

The bishop was not on his bed. I had the urge and strong desire to crawl under the carpet or floor if possible. Just then I heard a whimper coming from the other side of the room. I was suddenly aware of the depths and magnitude of my sinful state and wanted to get away from the unexpected visitor. I rolled off the bed and fell prostrate upon the floor. It was then that I realized the noise I had heard was the bishop who had already hit the floor and was also weeping and crying out to Jesus in prayer.

From time to time I would dare to peek out from the corners of my eyes. The heavenly light seemed to only grow brighter. As the light of the visitor grew lighter and brighter, it seemed that the anointing and glory of God also increased in our room. I was totally aware of my sinful nature and cried out to the Lord for mercy. This went on for about fifteen minutes. I was afraid to move, but occasionally peeped to see if the angel was still present. Each time I peeped, my eyes would hurt from the brightness of the light emitted from the angel.

Finally, I realized that the Lord was trying to do something. So I carefully addressed the Lord. I said, "Lord, what are You trying to do here tonight?" Instantly I had a supernatural revelation. It was not as though the angel spoke to me directly, but rather I had knowledge of the purpose of the angelic visitation. These words filled my mind: "You must be careful when you travel to Gulu. There will be great danger there. You must listen to what I say and be careful to do as I tell you. You must not travel northeast of Gulu." Instantly I saw a vision of a group of people riding in a white Jeep. The visitor went on: "You must fast and pray while you are in Gulu; no harm will befall you and your company. You will be tested; you must keep your focus and remember what I have spoken to you this night. Do not fear, God's presence will go before you and He will give unto thee rest."

When these words were related to me, I could begin to sense that the light was growing dimmer. As I raised my head, I saw the ball of light shimmer out. At the exact moment the ball of lightening disappeared, there was an audible "popping" sound; but the atmosphere in the room remained electric and energized. There was the smell of ozone floating in the air. It was like the smell that accompanies a thunderstorm, only much stronger and seemed to be mingled with frankincense.

It seemed as if I was glued to the floor. I was not able to move my body, so I waited there for a few minutes and contemplated what I had just experienced. A while later I rose up to my knees. The bishop was still on the floor. I suppose that the angel had been in the room for about twenty-five or thirty minutes. When I asked the bishop what he had experienced, he told me that he had seen the angel of God. His testimony is below.

## The Bishop's Testimony

*Evangelist Kevin and myself were enjoying a nice treatments at the Imperial Hotel as we had big plans to see the works of Brother Dunkin. We want to see how he is doing the work to help the orphans children in Uganda so we can also do the works with the many orphans in my home of Mwanza. Truly we do have many orphans in Tanzania that need much help.*

*We prayed and were preparing for the big trip up to Gulu; but is some kind dangerous, so we asked God for His blessing. Truly we need His help this time. While we were sleeping we did have heavenly visitor. It was most powerful. I am not able to stand so I did in fact get to the floor and I prayed for God's mercy. Truly the fear of God was with us that night. I stayed on the floor for sometimes and I stay with prayer. It was a long time before I have the strength to get up from my prayer, for fear I decide to keep with prayer until I am sure it is OK to rise up.*

*Up to now I have never had such a thing happen to me since I have serve the Lord Jesus. Evangelist Kevin said the heavenly visitor is come to help us for our trip to north Uganda, and I think maybe he is right also. For sure we did truly need help when we arrived into Gulu. We did discover that the LRA leader Joseph Kony was truly our neighbor at the hotel there in Gulu. Evangelist Kevin said that we should pray much, and we did pray with much of our heart.*

*One day we did see Kony face-to-face, and Evangelist Kevin did in fact speak to him. After that we decided that we truly needed to pray very much as Kony is now with us in the hotel. But our God is in fact greater and we did not have fear, but instead we have strong faith and did press on to preach at Pabo Camp. And we did see God do many signs and wonders among the people; there were many who did choose Jesus to be Savior. But now I am very glad to back in my home with my wife and my children; but by God we did get great victory and learn many things to help children in my city. Up to now we have for sure seen many thousand who have prayed to receive the Lord Jesus to be Savior as we labor together in the harvest fields of East Africa.*

## On to Gulu

The next day the team loaded up and drove to Gulu. I would like to share a brief account of those events as they bear out this angelic testimony. The first thing that happened was that there was a significant amount of discord that crept into the team. The bishop and I were asked to stay in at the Acholi Hotel in the center of Gulu on Elizabeth Road. Upon entering the hotel, I noticed that there were a lot of international media and NGOs present, including the NATO, WHO, The Red Cross, BBC, and others. I also noticed that there were Ugandan National Troops stationed all around the hotel compound. They had mounted fifty caliber machine guns on the wall near the entrance. The bishop and I talked about our surroundings. The Acholi was a hive of activity.

That evening we went to one of the camps for the children of the night to preach the Gospel to them. Since there was a cease-fire in effect, there were only about 1200 children on hand. We were told the number at this one camp was usually around 4000. That night several of the children prayed to receive Jesus Christ as Savior. Many others were healed as the team prayed for the sick. Six deaf children had their deaf ears open and were able to hear for the first time.

The next morning the bishop and I made our way to break-fast at the cafeteria at the hotel. In the courtyard we saw a reporter for the BBC and she was conducting an interview with a dignified Ugandan man. It turned out that he was a member of the government. I saw two English speaking journalists having breakfast and asked them why there was such a buzz and so many reporters and NGOs present at the hotel. One of the reporters asked me if I had read the paper, which I had not. So he began to tell me that there had been a major breakthrough with the LRA and there was a real chance that there would be a lasting peace agreement. The army was surrounding the hotel because Joseph Kony had surrendered to Ugandan troops that morning and they were bringing him there to talk with Ugandan officials.

At that time Joseph Kony was one of the leaders of the Lord's Resistance Army. He is alleged to be a truly evil man who has been responsible for thousands of murders and many other atrocities in Northern Uganda and the Sudan. Kony was a man who struck terror in the heart of most Ugandans. Kony is a self-proclaimed spokesperson of God and touts himself as a spirit medium. Kony also says that God speaks through him via the Holy Spirit. The problem with these claims is that Kony is involved in barbarous and grisly crimes.

## Press Release About Kony-Ugandan Peace Talks

*The elusive leader of a brutal 19-year Ugandan rebellion held his first formal peace talks with government officials, giving a boost to efforts to end a conflict that has swept up children and killed and maimed civilians. Joseph Kony, leader of the Lord's Resistance Army, shook hands with a delegation of 160 officials and lawmakers from northern Uganda and representatives of non-governmental organizations before three hours of talks Monday...inside the Congolese border. The camp was decorated in palm leaves as a sign of peace. Journalists were taken there, but were not told exactly where they were, and were not allowed to use their cell phones until they were returned to Sudan. "For meaningful talks to continue there must be a cessation of hostilities," the*

165

*rebels said in a statement after the talks. Kony had been expected to turn up for the talks Sunday....*

*Before Monday's talks, Kony met informally with some Ugandan government officials at a secret location Sunday night, said Walter Ochora, the top administrator of the northern Uganda district of Gulu, which has borne the brunt of Kony's rebellion. "It was very positive ... The man wants peace," Ochora told The Associated Press. He said Kony had been in poor health, coughing blood, but was feeling better. The Lord's Resistance Army is made up of the remnants of a rebellion that began after Ugandan President Yoweri Museveni took power in 1986. Its political agenda is unclear. But it has set up rear bases in Sudan and Congo, and has been accused of attacking civilians and threatening stability in those countries. It is known for abducting thousands of children, forcing them to become fighters, servants or concubines. Thousands of civilians have died in the conflict and more than 1 million have been forced to flee their homes. Kony is under indictment by the International Criminal Court, but Museveni has offered to protect him if the LRA agrees to give up its weapons. The rebels, however, have demanded that they be incorporated into Uganda's national army. New York-based Human Rights Watch denounced all calls for amnesty, saying international law rejects impunity for "genocide, war crimes, crimes against humanity and torture." - This statement was taken from a press release by the Associated Press.[1]*

As it turned out the secret location may have been the Acholi Hotel!

Even as I was speaking to the English journalists, the Ugandan national troops were busy enforcing the hotel perimeter. When I asked the two gentlemen if they know why this was in progress, they told me that Kony was due to arrive at any moment. There had been death threats against Kony because he had surrendered to the government and was attending the peace talks that were being held in the hotel. When the bishop and I finished our breakfast, we returned to our room. Along the way we saw that marksmen were being deployed into the trees inside of the hotel and there were now armed troops patrolling the perimeter of the hotel both inside and out. Armored cars were rumbling outside the gates as we left the hotel on our way to minister to the children that morning. Still, I had a peace remembering the words of the angel from the previous evening. Indeed, I had an unexplainable peace and was not concerned with the current events.

That afternoon we visited several ministries in Gulu. After the day was complete, we returned to the hotel to find that the troops and security had only increased. When we walked through the courtyard to our rooms, we were stopped by armed troops. They quickly came to attention as we turned on the sidewalk to our rooms, and they began to interrogate the bishop in Swahili. They demanded to see our room keys, and that seemed to placate them. We wondered why they had been stationed near our rooms, but we put it aside. We agreed to meet for dinner after we got cleaned up.

At dinner we discussed the events that were unfolding around us. We had been told that Joseph Kony had indeed surrendered and was being held prisoner in the hotel. That certainly made the presence of all of the additional troops and international new media more understandable. By now we had met some of the victims of the LRA. We met young children whose ears, hands, or lips had been cut off. We were introduced to adolescent girls who had been raped and who had escaped walking for days through the bush seeking asylum to have their unwanted baby. As we talked about the atrocities that we had seen, a passion began to well up from the depths of my spirit.

## A Face of Pure Evil

I told the bishop that since Kony was in the hotel, I was going too fast and pray for the Lord to touch him and to do something about the atrocities and the LRA. I boldly told the bishop, "If I see Kony here, I am going to preach the Gospel to him"! He chuckled and smiled, and I laughed as well. It was a way for us to break the uncomfortable feeling of the seriousness and tension of the situation. The next afternoon we were scheduled to travel to Pabo for the crusade meeting. The bishop and I decided to retire to our separate rooms and pray. I informed him that I would be staying in the hotel the next morning and not traveling with the team. I hoped to pray as I had promised and to also seek the will of the Lord for the Pabo crusade.

The next morning the bishop came to get me to come and sit with him for breakfast and discuss the crusade plans. Although I was fasting I did take some juice, and we talked and fellowshipped before he was to leave. After breakfast the bishop and I walked together back to our room. As we turned onto the sidewalk leading to our rooms, there was a flurry of activity. Just as I reached my door, a uniformed soldier suddenly jumped to attention and leveled an AK-47 at our bellies. The bishop's eyes became as big as saucers, and I suddenly had a queasy feeling in my stomach. He held his hands up and quickly conversed with the soldier in Swahili, and he lowered his weapon.

At that same moment there was an order barked out in Swahili. Suddenly the door next to my room burst open and a second soldier stepped out holding a pistol in his hand. I was totally unprepared for what happened next. In one fluid motion three more soldiers stepped out surrounding a tall black man in fatigues. The soldiers flanked the man, and he took two steps and was standing directly in front of me. At that unexpected instant I came face-to-face with evil incarnate. He slowly and deliberately looked at me from the top of my head to the souls of my feet. I could feel his contempt for me, and he was so close that I could smell his horrible breath. It was Joseph Kony.

I froze for a moment. Then I said, "Hello, sir." Kony sneered at me, and stared at me in the eye for just one moment. His face was full of hatred and contempt. I was looking directly into the eyes of pure evil. Then I thought to myself, "This is my chance to witness to Kony." However, all that proceeded out of my mouth was, "*Mungu aukia beriki, mesey.*" Translated from Swahili it means: "May God give His blessings to you, sir." The captain of the troops shouted something and the group pushed by as I turned the key and stepped into my room with the bishop close behind.

## Shaking

We were speechless for a moment. Then a great smile creased the face of the bishop. He laughed and said, "You have really given Kony a good sermon." We both laughed nervously. I was a little concerned that Kony was living in the room directly between the bishop and me. We talked for a few moments, and he said that it was time for him to prepare to leave for the morning. I was tempted to go as I was now uncomfortable with my new neighbor. Before the bishop left, I told him that we should both be praying much while we were in such a close proximity to Kony. He agreed and said that he would surely be joining me in prayer when he returned that morning before we left that afternoon for the crusade at Pabo. I told my friend good-bye and closed the door. It was then that I noticed my hands were shaking. I laughed; but it was not really funny.

I lay down on my bed and began to pray. I was restless so I rose up and began to pace and pray. It was then that I saw the soldiers through the rear window of my room. They were patrolling back and forth behind my room. In my mind I kept remembering what the Brits had told us: "There was a death threat and bounty placed on Kony's head." I looked at the walls and wondered if they were thick enough to withstand a grenade meant for Kony. I really began to pray. After an hour or so I remembered that the Lord has not given me a spirit of fear, but a spirit of power, of love, and a sound mind (2 Timothy 1:7). I recalled what the angel that manifested into our room at Imperial Botanical Beach Hotel had told me; "You will be tested; you must keep your focus and remember what I have spoken to you this night. Do not fear, God's presence will go before you and will He give unto thee rest." Yes, exactly, rest. That is what I needed.

I decided to lie down and to try to catch a short nap. I did indeed doze off. However, a short time later I was awakened by a loud pop, pop, pop, pop, pop, pop sound. My God, I thought. That is gun fire. I rolled off the bed onto the tile floor seeking to stay low and avoid being hit by a stray bullet. Pop, pop, pop, pop, pop, pop. They were firing again! Then I heard some men talking. I thought they did not seem to be very concerned with the gunfire, or this attack. I crawled over to the window and slowly raised my head up just enough to look outside. Slowly I rose up on my feet to get a better look. The soldiers were working on a room about thirty yards away. Pop, pop, pop echoed the sound from the sledge hammer as the workers drove a spikes into the wall. I burst out laughing at myself. What my sleeping mind thought were gunshots were actually blows from the sledge hammer. I spent a restless morning in the room praying for the crusade and asking the Lord to intervene with the LRA and Kony.

Later after lunch the bishop came to get me. The team had come to take us to Pabo for the crusade. The bishop was very excited and had our trusty bullhorn and fresh batteries. He had been informed that the pastors at Pabo were expecting a big crowd. We may see thousands saved this day! Praise God! I grabbed my preach bag and quickly followed the bishop to the jeep. The team was waiting. They were in a hurry, as we were running late. We jumped into the jeep and were off to Pabo.

## A White Jeep

We had driven about fifteen miles from Gulu when suddenly the Holy Spirit asked me a question. The Lord asked; "Where are you?" Instantly I knew what the Lord was saying. I had disregarded the instructions that the angel had given us in Entebbe: "You must be careful when you travel to Gulu. There will be great danger there. You must listen to what I say, and be careful to do as I tell you. You must not travel northeast of Gulu." I had also seen the vision of a group of people riding in a white Jeep. "You must fast and pray while you in the northeast; no harm befall you and your company. You will be tested; you must keep your focus and remember what I have spoken to you this night." "Oh, Lord, please forgive me, and help us," my mind screamed.

Here I was riding in a white Jeep. It was the same one I had seen in the vision. After about fifteen more minutes of travel on the rough road, I mustered up the courage to ask the driver Jerry a question: "Hey, Jerry, can you tell me what direction we are traveling?" He responded, "Sure we are just about thirty minutes from Pabo; we are going roughly northeast." I purposed to be strong and of good courage. Sure the angel had told me not to travel in a white jeep and not to go northeast; but how bad could it really be?

About that time we crested a small hill and rounded a curve surrounded by thick bushes. The Jeep suddenly screeched to a swift halt. Just as I was about to ask what was going on, I saw several Ugandan soldiers running at the jeep with their AK-47s primed and pointed at us. Then I heard a mechanical sound. Looking behind the soldiers, I saw an armored personnel carrier with a .50 caliber machine gun mounted to the top. It had just swiveled and the barrel was pointed at our white jeep. Soon the jeep was surrounded, and our driver Jerry said not to worry as he thrust his hands into the air. My friend told everyone in the jeep not to say a word, and for God's sake not to take any pictures.

Jerry and the captain of the troops had an animated discussion for several minutes. It seemed that the men wanted to have a case of the sodas we had tied to the luggage rack on top. In addition to this we were told that we should return to Gulu because the LRA had been seen moving through the area and that the army could not guarantee our safety. Jerry agreed to give the troops some soda, and after that was completed we continued on our way. It did not make me feel any better that the operator of the .50 caliber machine gun followed our progress by aiming the weapon in our direction as we drove away.

When we arrived at Pabo, we drove to a pastors meeting and were told that the witch doctors had been opposing the crusade. They had promised to curse anyone from Pabo who attended the meeting. Even worse they said that they would turn anyone attending over to LRA informants within the PDC. We were also told that death threats had been made against the preacher. "Oh great!" I thought. I was now wishing more than ever that I had remembered the angel's warning and obeyed!

We had a fellowship dinner with many of the Christians of Pabo. Then we were treated to a worship session. After worship we got into the white Jeep and rode to the place designated for the crusade. Instead of having 20,000 or more as we had hoped, there was only about 1,500 people on the grounds. Immediately when I stepped out of the Jeep my foot landed upon something. I looked down to see that I had stepped directly on a fetish. It was the carcass of a dead animal that the witch doctors had used in an incantation to curse the grounds the previous night. No one had dared to touch it to remove it from the grounds for fear of coming under the curse it signified. But here I was standing on this fetish with my left foot and smelling the foul demonic odor it emitted. "Jesus! Help!"

Nonetheless, the bishop and I were courageous. In my heart I asked the Lord for forgiveness for being disobedient. And I told the Lord that if I were to die today for preaching His Gospel, I was willing to be poured out like a drink offering for Him. However, I asked that He would grant that I would be able to lead at least 1000 people to Jesus as Savior and that He would glorify Himself by releasing mighty miracles here in Pabo. We took our bullhorns and climbed up to the makeshift platform and began to preach. God was so faithful. We saw many who were healed and set free, and it was estimated that several hundred people did pray to receive Jesus as Savior in that meeting at Pabo. God did amazing miracles at this outreach—the blind saw, the deaf heard, many tumors dissolved, and the Kingdom of Heaven invaded this stronghold of darkness in Pabo.

## The Sobering Consequences of Disobedience

The team was forced to make a quick retreat from Pabo that evening. As the crusade was winding down, there were men from another religion who had come to stone us. We all quickly said our good-byes to the pastors and began the long drive back to Gulu. We needed to reach the checkpoint by dusk or we would be forced to spend the night in Pabo. We enjoyed a hurried and dangerous ride back to Gulu. We crossed the checkpoint with just moments to spare and arrived back in Gulu safe and sound.

That night I was demonically attacked in my sleep. As a matter of fact, a strong demonic oppression settled upon my mind, and I fought to keep sickness from manifesting in my body. I believe that by disobeying the Lord and disregarding the angelic direction, I had opened a door for the enemy to oppress me. The next morning we were scheduled to leave Gulu. This too turned out to be a great blessing, as the shaky cease-fire fell apart.

The night before the LRA had raided a nearby village raping, pillaging, and plundering. Several children had been taken, and the front page of a local newspaper showed a large photo of six young women who had been tortured. The LRA had cut their lips off as a symbol of what would happen to those who informed against their movements and actions. The newspaper was a sickening reminder and display of the horrors that are for the most part forgotten by the Western world. We would never see such a photo in a Western newspaper. It is better that we ignore such travesties and continue in our comfortable lifestyles.

I fought this oppression and demonic dreams for about four months after returning from Uganda. It was not until Kathy and I traveled to North Carolina from Kansas City that I was set free. Let me stress the importance of this. This strong demonic oppression was working on my mind to quit the ministry. I had almost come to the point to agree with the lie. I was being physically attacked, and I was being tormented in my dreams by this same demonic force. I had just about given up.

## The Prophets

While we were in Moravian Falls my friend John Macgirvin suggested that we visit Bob Jones. He was at this time holding cell group meetings in his home close to Moravian Falls, in Statesville, North Carolina. John is a good friend of Mr. Jones. Kathy and I decided to go at the leading of the Holy Spirit. I sensed that the Lord "had something" for us there.

Bob is and was a wonderful man of God, and I truly enjoyed listening to him share. He was speaking about the eye of God among other things. At the end of the meeting, Bob Jones pointed out Kathy and me and asked us to stand up. There were about forty or so people in Bob's home that night. He said; "I am wanna to pray for you." I thought; "Alright, this is great!" But what happened next took me off guard.

As I stood before Bob Jones that evening, he said,

*Boy, I see a demon's done followed you back from Africa... That's right, ain't it? I see him sneakin' around over there... You been to Africa lately, have ya?*

I told him that I got back about four months before. Bob went on,

*That devil is trying to get you to lay down your call... You can't do that, friend... God really has a strong call on*

*your life. That is right... I see more than that on ya too... No... if you lay down that call that would be like a sin. No... the Lord has plans for ya, son... That thing has been lyin' to ya... I can see that it has been whisperin' in your ear... telling you that it is no use.... that ya ain't makin' no difference. Boy, that is a lie straight from the pits of hell... That means that you are makin' a big difference... The devil is tryin' to stop what the Lord has planned to work through you... No, you can't stop. God is callin' ya to preach the Gospel of the Kingdom and ta heal the sick. You got a real anointin' for miracles on ya.*

Mr. Jones then laid hands upon Kathy and me for impartation. He also prayed and prophesied over me and broke the power of the demonic curse that was oppressing me. I immediately felt a great freedom and a release. From that day forward I was free from that oppression. One thing I do know is that by my disobedience I had placed myself out of the Lord's perfect will. I allowed myself to be in a position that opened the door for the enemy to take pot shots at me and seek to destroy me and the ministry that the Lord has laid upon my heart. I endured about 120 days of torment that was totally unnecessary had I just listened to the angel and not traveled northeast of Gulu. The Lord has sought to protect us by giving us a warning through the angelic ministry. I am reminded of how the Holy Spirit warned Paul not to travel to Bithynia in Acts 16:7-9.

Let that be a lesson to you. Obedience is better than sacrifice (1 Samuel 15:22). I am in no way comparing myself or my experiences to the prophet Daniel or the Apostle Paul, but what I want to convey to you is that the Lord still uses angels to give His saints and friend's important messages and guidance. It is not necessary to be some kind of spiritual giant to experience angelic ministry.

What is important is the condition of our hearts. The Lord is more interested in our hearts than our hands. In other words, the Lord would prefer that we strive to become His friends and be obedient to His guidance rather than strive to be anointed to be some kind of popular miracle worker or minister. I once heard it said: "It is better to be a well done good and faithful servant, than a half-baked preacher."

I believe that multitudes of God's friends will begin to encounter Godly angels like the one described in this testimony who will bring them messages for guidance and protection at this hour. Please remember that obedience *is* better than sacrifice.

If you have enjoyed reading these modern day testimonies of angelic visitations and other supernatural experiences, please look for the next book in this supernatural series; *Angelic Visitations and Other Supernatural Encounters Volume 2,* coming soon.

# Prayers

## Prayer of Salvation

Perhaps you would like to be born again and receive Jesus as your Lord and Savior now. Just pray this prayer out loud:

*Father God, I believe that Jesus Christ is the Savior or Messiah. I believe that Jesus is the only begotten Son of God and that He died upon the cross to make payment for my sins. I believe that Jesus was buried in an unused grave, but that after three days He rose again to conquer death and sin. Lord, because I was born a human being I was born a sinner. Lord, I ask You to forgive my sins now in the name of Jesus Christ of Nazareth. God cover my sins with the blood of Jesus; forgive me now. Amen.*

# Prayer of Impartation and Activation and of 20/20 Spiritual Vision

*At this moment I bless my God and the Father of my Lord Jesus Christ, who has blessed me with every spiritual blessing in the heavenly places in Christ. And I pray that the God of my Lord Jesus Christ, the Father of glory, may give unto me the spirit of wisdom and revelation in the knowledge of Him. Lord, I ask in the name of Jesus Christ of Nazareth that the eyes of my spirit might receive supernatural understanding and become enlightened.*

*I ask, Father, that I may know what is the hope of Your calling upon my life and comprehend what are the riches of the glory of the Lord's inheritance in me. Lord, reveal to me what is the exceeding greatness of Your power toward me, because I believe. Lord, release to me the revelatory understanding according to the working of Your mighty power which You worked in Christ Jesus as He rose from the dead and You seated Him at Your right hand in the heavenly places.*

*Father, You placed the Lord Jesus far above every principality and power and might and dominion and every name that is named, not only in this age but also in that which is to come. Lord, make known to me all of the fullness and unsearchable riches of Christ. Help me to see and comprehend what is the fellowship of the mystery, which from the beginning of the ages has been hidden in God who created all things through Jesus Christ*

*For this reason I bow my knees to the Father of our Lord Jesus Christ, from whom the whole family in heaven and earth is named. And I ask You, Lord, that You would grant unto me according to the riches of His glory, that I may be strengthened with might through Your Spirit in my soul and inner man. Lord, I pray that Christ may dwell in my heart through faith; that I will become rooted and grounded in the love of God.*

*Lord, I ask that I might comprehend with all the saints what is the width and length and depth and height— and to personally know and experience the love of Christ, which passes all knowledge, that I may be filled with all the fullness of God. And I thank You, Lord, who is able to do exceedingly abundantly above all that I can ask or think, according to the power of Your Spirit that works within me.*

*Lord, I thank You now that You are releasing to me the spirit of wisdom and revelation of Your Kingdom and the mighty effectual working of your power in my life, spirit, soul, and body. Thank You, Lord, that You are opening the eyes of my heart and helping me to see and discern the fullness of your Kingdom as it manifests in my life. And to You, Lord, be all the glory in the church by Christ Jesus to all generations, forever and ever. Amen.*

# Prayer of Reception

*Lord, I choose to believe to receive. Father, in Jesus' name, I purpose in my heart to believe to receive the prophetic promises that the Holy Spirit has placed into these pages. Lord, I am ready, I am willing, and I choose to receive everything that You are seeking to release to me from the Kingdom of Heaven though this book.*

*Holy Spirit, I ask that You would guide me and teach me. Lord, I ask that You would open my spiritual eyes and activate my spiritual ears to see and hear in a Christlike way. Lord Jesus, You said that to me it has been given and granted to know the hidden mysteries of the Kingdom of Heaven. Today, Lord, I choose to revive those blessings and revelations that You have hidden for me in the Holy Scriptures. Help me to see the keys to unlock the hidden mysteries of Your word and of Your Kingdom to me now. Lord, let Your Kingdom come into my life on earth as it is in heaven today.*

*I ask You to reveal to me the secrets and hidden mysteries that eye has not seen nor ear heard. Lord, I ask You to ignite my heart by Your Spirit and let the Kingdom of Heaven enter into my heart. Reveal to me the mysteries and the secret things that You have prepared for those who love You. I ask You, Father, in the name of Jesus, to reveal the fellowship of the mysteries and the unsearchable riches found in Christ to me. Reveal them to my spirit. O Lord, open my eyes to see the mysteries hidden in the Kingdom of Heaven. Lord, help me to discern the manifold wisdom of God. Lord, I am asking You to give me eyes to see and ears to hear in a new and supernatural way. In the name of Jesus Christ of Nazareth I pray. Amen!*

## Prayer to Activate Godly Discernment

*Lord, I ask You to reveal to me the secrets and hidden mysteries that eye has not seen nor ear heard. Lord, I ask You to ignite my heart by Your Spirit and let the Kingdom of Heaven enter into my heart. Reveal to me the mysteries and the secret things that You have prepared for those who love You. I ask You, Father, in the name of Jesus, to reveal the fellowship of the mysteries and the unsearchable riches found in Christ to me. Reveal them to my spirit. O Lord, open my eyes to see the mysteries hidden in the Kingdom of Heaven. Lord, help me to discern the manifold wisdom of God. Lord I am asking You to give me eyes to see and ears to hear in a new and supernatural way. In the name of Jesus I pray. Amen!*

## Dangerous Prayer

*Lord, if You are real, then I want to see You. I want to experience Your love and glory first hand. Lord, I want to be like that guy called Saul in Acts 9. Yes, Lord! Let a light from heaven shine upon me! Jesus, come and speak to me Face-to-face, like a man does to a friend.*

*Jesus, if You are real, then I want You to come and visit me. I want to be knocked off of my horse. I want you to appear to me like You appeared to that dude Saul. Show me a light from heaven! Reveal Yourself to me, Jesus. Let me be knocked off of my high horse! Let me have to get up from the road picking gravel from between my teeth. Lord, anoint and empower some guy like Ananias to come and lay his hands upon me that I might may receive my sight and have my spiritual vision activated! O Lord, that I might be filled with the fullness of Your Holy Spirit. Open my eyes to see You, Lord Jesus. Open my ears to hear You speak to me, my God! Help me to see and hear in a new and supernatural way. In Jesus name I pray. Amen!*

## Prayer to See and Hear in a New Way

*Father, Your word says that the testimony of Jesus is the spirit of prophesy. So, Lord, I ask You now to begin to help me to see in a new way. Lord, in the name of Jesus Christ, I ask You, Father, that I would begin to hear in a new way. Holy Spirit, I ask for You to guide and to teach me today. Holy Ghost, help me to learn to see and to hear in a new way. Lord, help to reveal to my spirit what Jesus desired for me to understand when He taught in Luke 8:18:* "Take heed how you hear. For whoever has, to him more will be given." *Lord, I am asking that more will be given to me to help me to hear the way that You wish for me to hear of God. And right now I thank You, Lord, for opening up my spiritual ears to hear and opening up my spiritual eyes to see in new and amazing ways. In Jesus' name I pray. Amen!*

## Prayer for Boldness to See and Hear in a New Way

*Father, in Jesus' name I ask that You grant to Your servant boldness to see and hear the way that You want me to see and hear. It is right in Your sight, O God, to listen and to hear You more clearly rather than listen to the doctrine of man. Lord, I ask that You open up the seer realms to me so that I am empowered by Your Spirit to see and hear clearly from Your Kingdom. Then I shall decree: "For I cannot but speak the things which I have seen and heard." In Jesus' name, I pray. Amen.*

## Prayer for Manifestations of the Kingdom

*Lord, I thank You that Your Kingdom is a supernatural place. Today I choose to recognize that You created the heavens and the earth. The earth is Yours, Lord, and it is a supernatural place. Today, Lord, I ask You in the mighty name of Jesus to help me to discern and perceive the supernatural aspects of the terrestrial or earthly realms. Give me eyes to see and discern the places and times where You open the heavens over my life. In Jesus' name I pray. Amen.*

# Prayer for the Cleansing of the Heart
## (Based on Psalm 51)

*Father, today in the mighty name of Jesus Christ of Nazareth, I ask You, Lord, that You would search my heart. Lord, search my inner parts; and through the power and ministry of the precious Holy Spirit, I ask that You would reveal anything that is hidden in the chambers of my heart. Lord, shine the light of Your Kingdom upon me and uncover any hidden agendas or hidden sins that I am not aware of. Lord, reveal any idols that I have unwittingly allowed to reign in my heart. Lord, I ask that You would heal and deliver me right now, in the name of Jesus Christ. Lord, I pray that You would minister to me according to the precepts of Psalm 51. Lord Jesus, wash me thoroughly from my iniquity and cleanse me from my sin. I acknowledge my transgressions, and my sin is always before me. Against You, You only, O Lord, have I sinned, and done evil in Your sight. Lord, may You be found just when You speak and blameless when You judge me, O God.*

*You are a merciful God. Remember, O Lord, that I was brought forth in iniquity and in sin my mother conceived me. Reveal Your truth and Your nature in my inward parts, and in the hidden parts may You allow me to know wisdom. Purge me with hyssop, and I shall be clean. Wash me with the blood of Jesus and I shall be whiter than snow. Make me hear with joy and gladness that even my bones may rejoice in You alone, Lord. Hide*

*Your face from my sins, and blot out all my iniquities. And I pray in the name of Jesus that You would create in me a clean heart, O God, and renew a steadfast spirit within me. Cast me not away from Your presence, and do not take Your Holy Spirit from me. Lord, I ask that You restore to me the fullness of the joy of Your salvation, and uplift and heal me by the power of Your generous Spirit. Amen!*

## Prayer of the Father's Blessing

*Father, You promised to bless us with every blessing in the heavenly places. And today, heavenly Father, I ask that You would pour out upon me a Father's blessing. Father, in Jesus' name I pray that You would open the windows of heaven and release Your good treasure to me. Pour out Your grace and favor upon my life. It is Your good pleasure to give me the Kingdom. And today, Lord, I am asking that the Kingdom of Heaven would come upon my life in a fresh and new way. O Father, I ask that You would bless me indeed! Amen.*

## Prayer of Covering

*Lord Jesus, thank You for Your blood. I cover myself in Your blood right now, and I thank You that Your blood is the most powerful substance upon the earth. Thank You, Lord, for washing me and totally forgiving me from by sins with Your own blood. Lord Jesus, today I recognize that by the power of Your blood, I have been transformed into a king and royal priest. And I thank You, Lord, that these privileges open up the doors and gates of the heavenly realms and make a way for me to minister to my God and Father. Thank You, Lord Jesus, because You have redeemed us to God by Your blood. Thank You, Lord, that I may ascend into the hill of the Lord. As I mature and learn to walk in greater levels of holiness and purity each day, I ask that You would give me further revelation of what it means to bind on earth and that I might also learn how to loose Your Kingdom upon the earth and understand the mysteries of what will be loosed in heaven. In Jesus' name I pray. Amen.*

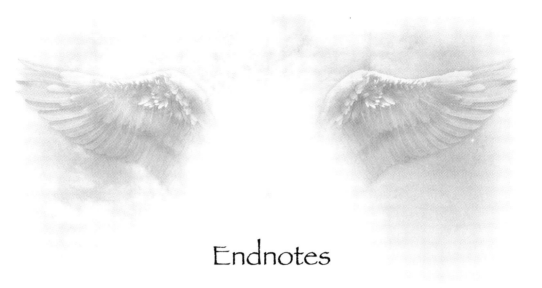

# Endnotes

1. "LRA Kony holds first formal peace talks with Ugandan officials," *Sudan Tribune*, Tuesday, August 1, 2006, http://www.sudantribune.com/spip.php?article16887 (accessed May 22, 2015).

# Unlocking the Hidden Mysteries of the Seer Anointing

This book contains the teachings the revelations that the Lord has given Kevin over the last 12 year about the seer anointing. We are living in a God ordained moment of time when the seer realm is being released by grace to God's friends (whosoever). This book is designed to help God's people unlock the hidden mysteries of the seer anointing in their lives by understanding the idiosyncrasies of the seer anointing in a Christ centered and sound biblical manner. It is a very through biblical teaching that also is replete with dozens of prayers of activation for the reader (seers).

$20.00

**SALE $15.00**

# Unlocking the Hidden Mysteries of the Seer Anointing II
## *The Blessings of Psalm 24*

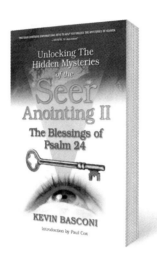

In the new book, *Unlocking the Hidden Mysteries of the Seer Anointing and the Blessings of Psalm 24*, Kevin Basconi continues to open up the hidden mysteries of the seer anointing. This book is a sequel to Kevin's first book on the seer anointing. In it he shares a set of powerful testimonies of angelic visitations and supernatural experiences that were released from the realms of Heaven. On February 25th, 2014 Kevin had a powerful visitation of the spirit of wisdom and revelation and was launched into a seer experience. The Seer Anointing and the Blessings of Psalm 24 is a MUST READ! This amazing new book is a great read and it is full of Kingdom keys and revelation from Psalm 24 and other places that can help you to activate and accelerate the seer gift and anointing in your life.

~~$20.00~~

**SALE $15.00**

# Unlocking the Hidden Mysteries
## of the Seer Anointing III
### *The Shaking & The Arising*

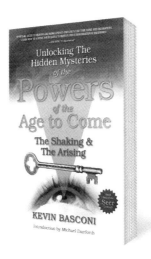

Spiritual gates to heaven are being opened for God's end-time sons and daughters. Kevin Basconi was taken to heaven to teach you how to access these gates!

–SID ROTH, Host, "It's Supernatural!"

~~$20.00~~

**SALE $15.00**

This book was prepared for printing by

## King of Glory Printing & Publishing

Our goal is to help unpublished authors facilitate printing of their manuscripts in a professional and economical way. If you have a manuscript you would like to have printed, contact us:

336-818-1210
or
828-320-3502

PO BOX 903
Moravian Falls, NC 28654

www.kingofgloryministries.org